THE
Mortgaged
Millionaire

THE Mortgaged Millionaire

**How Paying Off Your Mortgage First
Can Sentence You To A Lifetime Of Debt**

Nolan Matthias

IVP
InnerVoicePublishing.com

To order bulk quantities of this book please contact
customerservice@nolanmatthias.com

Published by InnerVoicePublishing.com
110-6650 Old Banff Coach Road
Calgary, Alberta, Canada
T3H 4J4

InnerVoicePublishing.com ISBN 978-0-9782512-1-5

Visit Nolan Matthias at www.nolanmatthias.com

Visit The Mortgaged Millionaire webpage and blog at
www.themortgagedmillionaire.ca

Library and Archives Canada Cataloguing in Publication

Matthias, Nolan, 1983-
    The mortgaged millionaire : how paying off your mortgage
first can sentence you to a lifetime of debt / Nolan Matthias.

ISBN 978-0-9782512-1-5

    1. Finance, Personal. 2. Investments. 3. Mortgage loans.
4. Debt. I. Title.

HG179.M3758 2012   332.024   C2011-908422-8

Disclaimer

The author and publisher have taken great care in preparing this book, however make no representations or warranties with respect to the accuracy or completeness of its content. The contents of this book should not be considered a substitute for professional financial advice. Please consult a financial professional before implementing any of the strategies described in this book. The author and publisher shall not be held liable for any loss of profit or any other financial damages, including but not limited to special, consequential, incidental, or other damages.

To my Mother and Father who taught me the value of a dollar and the power of compound interest. In other words, everything I know about money and finance.

Table of Contents

Acknowledgement

Three years, an all too familiar time frame. My first book, Golf Balls Don't Float, took three years to write. In the three years since it has been published, it has sold over 7,000 copies, all without ever touching the shelf of a bookstore. Like my first book, The Mortgaged Millionaire also took three years to write. These three years however, seemed significantly longer. The amount of time spent running numbers, researching, and fact checking, took nearly as much time as it took to write my entire first book. It seems that writing a book of the finance variety is considerably more complicated than writing that of the business/self-help variety. Consequently, it took many more people to complete this project than the last.

This time around my first acknowledgement belongs to my Mother, who laid the groundwork for every piece of financial knowledge and success that I have discovered thus far. I had a bank account before I had a school bag and an investment account before a textbook. I was trading stocks before high school, and had my first mortgage before the end of my first year of university. It was the opportunity to learn, play, and experiment with money long before I had any of my own

1

that taught me just how important financial education is.

To my Father, who passed along the genetic gene that codes for an entrepreneurial spirit, you are the reason why I have leaped when scared into the unknown of owning a business. You are also the reason that business became my hobby. It was the days as a child travelling with you to and from the office that sparked my interest in commerce. I will never forget those days.

To my wife Jen, who showed up in my life midway through the writing of this book, you could not have come at a better time. While I could have published this book sooner, it was you that encouraged me to wait until the time was right, and I thank you for that. The time is now right.

To Jessica Kluthe, you were a part of the last one, and an even bigger part of this one. Thank you for being the one who convinced me to move forward with this book when it could have just ended up being another idea that never got executed.

To Ron Stanners, thank you for helping me realize that there is no one-size-fits-all answer when it comes to finance. Thank you also for allowing me to develop and grow my business under your wing.

To Alice Chan, thank you for your feedback early on. You fed me with ideas that reshaped this book into what it is today.

To Meini Ickert, Kelly Neuber, and Bob Ord, I appreciate your support both prior to and after joining Mortgage Architects.

To Yousry Bissada, Ed Karthaus, Loren Cooke, Paul Grewal, Gord Ross, Gord Dahlen, Jim Murphy, and Mark Webb, you may not have realized it at the time, but individual conversations with each of you helped shape this book to what it is today.

Lastly, to Dr. Frank Atkins, thank you for telling me to "look out the window." It was that phrase that lead me to get my mortgage brokers license, even though my economics degree could have taken me so many other places.

To all of you, again, thank you.

Introduction

As I write the introduction to this book and reflect on where I was when this compilation of words, numbers, and insights started, I realize that everything in the mortgage industry has changed. When this journey started, the minimum down payment needed to avoid mortgage insurance was 25%; now, it is 20%. It used to be that the maximum amortization on a mortgage was 25 years; now, it is 30 – in the past few years, it has even been as high as 40. You used to have to put at least 5% down just to buy a house. Then, the banks and insurers made it possible to buy a house with no money down, only to retract those very products a couple of years later. However, there are still options if you don't have a down payment. The government got less restrictive on rental property purchases, and then, they got more restrictive. They have reduced the percentage of your home that you can refinance, eliminating the ability to use a home as a bank account, while also eliminating the ability to eradicate high risk expensive debt by folding it back into your mortgage. Things have gotten better, but they have also gotten worse, depending on what you are trying to do or where you stand.

I have thrown out no less than four chapters of this book and rewritten five, because every time I get close to publishing, the government would change something and render a portion of this book useless. However, I have continued to write, tweak, and refine, knowing that I would likely have to change things again in the future. I fully expect to have to amend and rewrite chapters after I publish this book, and I look forward to it. I look forward to creating new strategies, better strategies, that help mortgage borrowers understand how to use their mortgages to build wealth. I look forward to dispelling myths, like the ones propagated by so many banks, financial institutions, and mortgage brokers.

For the first time in history, banks have become more aggressive with their existing clientele. It used to be that a new client seemed to be treated better than one who had been with their bank for a long period of time. Renewal notices used to go out with sky-high rates attached in the hopes that the client would not try to negotiate, and profits would be maximized. Banks now realize that this practice is a losing proposition since clients are now better informed than ever before. Thank you, Internet! Instead, banks now have a new strategy: give clients what they want – low rates – and take away all of the things that they don't know they need. Slash the prepayment privileges, increase the payout penalties, and lock them in for 3 years unless they sell. Then, register the mortgage as a collateral mortgage so that they can't leave without paying a lawyer. Sure, they'll think they are getting a great rate, but they are getting what they pay for: a featureless mortgage.

Banks are taking away the features that have the potential to make you rich by making you think that your lower rate will make up for it. Not so fast though – you don't even realize they are taking these features away, because you don't know

6

you need them or even know why.

All of this change means one thing: good advice and expertise are now more important than ever. Understanding opportunity costs, how mortgages actually work, and a person's personality type are essential. If you don't understand these three things, then you are at a disadvantage. Additionally, don't just think you know how a mortgage works, because chances are that you don't know a thing about the intricacies of one of the most complex financial products an individual will ever have to deal with. Most people who have been in the mortgage industry for three or four years don't have an intimate knowledge of the intimate details. Like I said, advice and expertise are now more important than ever.

A Note On Financial Education

The type of financial guidance that has been handed out either by or to the Baby Boom Generation is comparable to that of a parent acting as a hockey coach. While a parent intuitively has a desire to see his or her child succeed, they may not have the coaching or hockey experience to develop their child into a superstar. No matter how much a parent reads, learns, or tries, a parent's advice cannot substitute or discount the advice of an actual hockey coach. Similarly, a parent's advice should not be a substitute for a financial professional's advice.

Theoren Fleury, the former NHL hockey star, touched on the importance of professional financial advice in a conversation with me several years ago. He said, "The emphasis on financial education in society is so minimal. I spent years playing hockey and made millions of dollars. I had the best coaching on the planet when it came to the skills that made me my money, yet no one even thought to try to teach me what to do with that money once I had earned it."

It is generally accepted that the best people to teach a child about money are the parents, not the child's teachers. This can lead to a vast array of learning methods, from detailed instruction to go-out-and-figure-it-out-yourself-type mentalities. However, a parent can help a child develop the foundation of their financial knowledge as early as a child can count. For instance, letting a child be the scorekeeper in board games like Monopoly, count the change in the jar on the dresser, or even roll pennies and dimes to understand how small change can add up are all ways to introduce money concepts. Yet, just as a parent can tie up their child's first pair of skates and bring them to the arena every Sunday for power skating lessons, there is a point where a parent exhausts their ability to be an effective hockey coach. Similarly, there is a point where a parent exhausts their ability to be an effective financial coach. Furthermore, financial concepts are more complex than understanding how to execute the perfect penalty kill. Unfortunately, Western educational systems are not setup to teach people how to become financially successful, putting the onus on parents to teach financial concepts which would be better taught through a structured educational system, a system where all children would have the opportunity to receive the same up-to-date information.

One child's parents may have the ability to instill money concepts, such as how to save and spend, while another child's parents may not even understand how to save money themselves or why it is important to do so. This creates an inequality in the potential for a child to be financially successful. In theory, the educational system is set up to provide the same skill sets to all children, which could contribute to these children earning their income and could be the difference between retiring at age 65 or at age 85. Every child who goes to school is given the same opportunity to learn the curriculum that can lead to higher education, which in turn, could potentially lead to monetarily rewarding jobs, such as a lawyer or doctor. Yet, the ability to develop knowledge of how to survive financially after these positions are secured is not equivalent, given the fact that financial education is not a focus of the current educational system.

Slice's 2009 reality television show "Til Debt Do Us Part," which features many young families in serious financial crisis, attests to the fact that there needs to be a formalized method of financial education. A high school education should not only include the ability to understand and calculate compound interest, but also teach practical applications and the importance of this very concept. Our educational system teaches students subjects from Language Arts to mathematics so that they can earn money by securing careers. In other words, traditional education teaches students the basic skills that lead to the ability to perform tasks which can earn them income, yet this education stops short of teaching students what to do with those earnings.

With no structured financial education, the typical financial advice has always been to save a certain percentage of your income, and pay down debt as fast as possible, even though this may not be the best advice. This can be useful advice depending on whom it is given to, but it is advice that is usually only considered and often not acted upon until it is too late. Furthermore, people who give this type of advice don't often consider that one blanket piece of counsel is not necessarily the best advice for all types of financial situations. Just as everyone wears different sized hockey skates, everyone requires different financial guidance in order to build wealth—which again, is why good advice is so important.

Good advice is what I hope to deliver to you in the pages
that follow.

Section 1
The Theories

1

Forget Everything
The Game Has Changed

Galileo Galilei

In 1632, astronomer Galileo Galilei was ordered to appear before the Holy Office in Rome to defend his controversial text, Dialogue Concerning the Two Chief World Systems. His work compared the Copernican system, which theorized that the Earth circled the Sun, with the Ptolemaic system, which was the mainstream belief that the Earth was the center of the Universe. A year later, Galileo stood trial for his dissenting, yet accurate, beliefs and advocacy of Copernicanism.

Galileo was not tried because he had created the theory that the Earth circled the Sun; instead, Galileo faced condemnation because he had discovered celestial evidence to prove the theory. With the use of a telescope, Galileo observed that much in the same way that the Earth's moon orbits the Earth, Jupiter's four moons orbited that planet. He used this scientific observation to argue in favor of Nicholas Copernicus's theory that the Earth circled the Sun, a theory which had been dismissed six decades earlier. Scientists and religious authorities had fiercely rejected Copernicanism as a result of its conflict with contemporary religious beliefs that the Earth was at the center of the Universe.

Importantly, there was no scriptural evidence that the Earth was the center of the universe. Yet, believers of this contemporary theory cited Psalms 93:1 and 96:10 that suggested that the world stood still. Galileo urged individuals not to take biblical phrases concerning the Earth literally and, instead, to consider such phrases as metaphors. This suggestion threatened the power of the Established Church and angered religious authorities; as a result, Galileo was convicted of heresy.

Sentenced to spend the rest of his life under house arrest and have his book added to the Index of Forbidden Books, Galileo was ordered to recant, and he spent his dying days speaking of his beliefs only in a hypothetical sense. It was not until more than 200 years after Galileo's death that his book was removed from the Index of Forbidden Books and that the theory was accepted as scientific fact. The Catholic Church did not officially acknowledge that the Earth did not "stand still" in a literal sense until 1992.

This brief summary of a complex story reveals three important parallels synonymous with the arguments that will be made in subsequent sections of this book. First, established beliefs are hard to argue even if there is clear evidence to support opposing views. Second, the indoctrinated will defend their position even if decisive proof is presented. Third, even though there may be long periods of persecution, ideas that are developed in good faith and supported by evidence will almost always be accepted as truth.

370 Years Later

Several years ago, a good friend, who happened to also be a client, challenged me. He asked me whether he should make a 5% or a 25% down payment on the property that he was in the process of buying. I emphatically answered 25%. Why was this my initial response? It was the only way of avoiding the 2-4% in CMHC fees (insurance required on all mortgages of 75% or more of the property value at the time) that it would cost him up front.

To paraphrase a discussion that will be considered in further detail later in this book, our conversation went as follows.

"If I took that extra 20% and used it as a down payment as opposed to other alternatives, what would it cost me?" he asked.

"Nothing, it would save you not only the CMHC fee, but also the interest you would have to pay on the excess money if you borrowed it," I replied.

"Are you sure about that?" he asked.

"Well, I guess you would, in theory, lose whatever interest you could earn on that money."

"Exactly!" he replied. "If that amount of interest was higher than the cost of borrowing, I would actually be losing money by putting more down, not saving money. Wouldn't you agree?"

However, I still was not sold. I was still stuck on the fact that he would be giving up that initial fee: an insurance premium designed to protect the bank, not the client. I argued for nearly 50 minutes, not because I had worked the numbers out myself and not because there wasn't distinct evidence against my opinion, but because all I had ever been told was to put as much money down as possible. I argued and dismissed his idea similar to the way in which the religious authorities dismissed Copernicus and Galileo: simply because my financial mentors had taught me that it was better to put more money down when buying a house, and up until this point, no one had ever questioned it. This idea had been established in my mind, but it was nothing more than a belief that I assumed to be correct.

Similar to the case of Galileo, there was clear evidence opposing my position. However, being one of the indoctrinated, I held my position even though there was a high probability that I was wrong. I argued from a position of ignorance simply because I believed what I had been told, not because I had evidence to back up my claim. Eventually, much like in the case of Galileo, I realized the opposing argument had validity, which led to the removal of my financial blinders and my acceptance that avoiding mortgage insurance isn't always the most lucrative financial option. Chapter 8 in this book, "Debating Mortgage Insurance," was derived from this very conversation.

The point to both of these short stories is to help you open your eyes to other lines of thinking so that we can break down the fallacies of personal finance and debt. Just as Galileo's convictions in his beliefs motivated him to fight an uphill battle, this book will do the same. We will explore the parallels between ideas such as "the world stands still," and "pay off your mortgage as fast as possible." Additionally, we will investigate how ideas passed along from generation to generation carry important wisdom but should not necessarily be accepted as facts. We will eliminate the perceptions that prevent us from building wealth, and replace them with realistic strategies that actually have the potential to help us accumulate assets and money over time.

The Homestead Mentality

In the instances of Galileo and of my friend, long standing beliefs and teachings stood in the way of new and better ideas. The simple act of passing along information from elder to junior over several decades was enough to prevent even the consideration of alternative possibilities when it came to both celestial evidence and mortgages; however, this is not unusual.

Limiting beliefs due to traditional wisdom are common. Take for example the four-minute mile. Until Roger Banister successfully ran a mile in less than four minutes, no one believed it was possible. Traditional wisdom had declared that the four-minute mile was impossible, because a mere few had tried it and failed. These few were considered the best of the best when it came to running; however, most of them had learned to run not with the intent of running a four minute mile but with the intent to win races. If winning a race only meant running faster than the next fastest person, and the next fastest person was someone who did not even come close to the four minute mark, then there was little need to run a mile that fast.

Tasking the fastest runners in the world to try and run a four minute mile ultimately resulted in all of them failing because their training had not been designed to run a mile that fast; it had been designed to win races. If the fastest runners in the world could not run a four minute mile, then most people assumed no one could do it. The fallacy that the four-minute mile was unachievable was then passed on from person to person, even though the majority of the people passing the information along had no concept of whether or not it was actually a reasonable task. That is until Roger Bannister came along and trained with the specific purpose of running a mile in under four minutes. He succeeded at reaching his goal, and he shattered the established belief system.

The societal habit of passing along information without personal understanding is why the "pay off your mortgage as fast as possible" ideology has taken priority over the "build wealth as fast as possible mentality." If you think about it, does it really make more sense to focus on paying off debt than it does to focus on building wealth? I personally do not think so.

However, several generations disagree, and they have passed on the traditional pay off your mortgage wisdom in the same manner that those who never even attempted to run a four-minute mile did. The lack of personal reflection and understanding of this concept, along with blind reiteration, has caused a massive misunderstanding of mortgages in our society that few have chosen to explore beyond unsubstantiated advice.

As a piece of advice, paying off your mortgage as fast as you can seems to make sense intuitively. If you pay off your mortgage, you will be debt free, have less monthly obligations, pay less interest, and no one can ever take your home from you. Baby Boomers and the generation prior typically share this belief and the belief that all debt is bad. Most Boomers will revert back to charts and calculations of the thousands of dollars that a person will pay over and above the purchase price of their homes in order to prove that mortgages are bad news. Like the belief that the world is the center of the Universe, however, this type of logic is passed on not because it is understood, but because it has been engrained, entrenched, and unchallenged.

Examining the generations prior to the Baby Boomers' demonstrates that the generations that so adamantly counseled the Baby Boomer Generation to pay off their mortgage quickly did so for much different reason than the Boomers might think. If you ask someone who had come of age before the 1930's their reason for paying off their mortgage, it usually has less to do with being debt free and more to do with earning income.

At this point in history, the proportion of rural residents to urban dwellers was much different. In 1901, 63% of the population lived in rural areas as opposed to only 20% today.

Year	Urban Population	Rural
1901	37%	63%
1911	45%	55%
1921	49%	51%
1931	54%	46%
1941	54%	46%
1951	62%	38%
1961	70%	30%
1971	76%	24%
1981	76%	24%
1991	77%	23%
2001	80%	20%
2011	80%	20%

*Source - Statistics Canada 2006 Census

Of those who lived in rural areas in the early 1900's, the majority derived their income from agriculture, either directly or indirectly. The importance of agriculture meant that, for many people, there was a correlation between their mortgage and their income. The land that farmers made mortgage payments on was more than just a place to live; it was where they grew the crops and bred the animals that earned them a living. In other words, a person's home, and more importantly their mortgage, was tied directly to their pay cheque. If a farmer failed to pay their mortgage, they ran the risk of losing their farm, which meant that they would also simultaneously lose their means of earning an income.

Conversely, a farmer who was mortgage free never risked losing his home or his income. Furthermore, a farmer who successfully paid off the mortgage on one piece of land could then purchase additional land by taking out a new mortgage. Because the first piece of land was completely paid off, it would always be secure, meaning the farmer would never have to worry about losing it, virtually guaranteeing that he would always be able to produce an income. The farmer would also have twice the earning power going towards paying off the additional mortgage, lowering the risk of not being able to make the payments on the additional land. Every time a mortgage was paid off, the farmer could buy an additional piece of land, further increasing his security, his economies of scale, and lowering the amount of time it would take to pay off each new mortgage. The only limitation would be the amount of land a farmer could physically harvest on his own.

The likelihood of earning income from a personal residence today is unlikely unless you are in fact a farmer by profession, which means that you must come up with other strategies in order to ensure security and wealth accumulation. The question is: does it still make sense to follow the mortgage advice of your grandparent's generation when your circumstances are so different? The simple answer is no.

Paying off a mortgage as fast as possible is a mistake for many individuals who do not directly earn income from their property. You need to ask yourself not how can you pay off your mortgage faster, but how can you use your money most effectively to build wealth and create security? In many cases, the answer is not to pay off your mortgage rapidly, but rather, the answer is to save and invest rapidly instead, putting away as much money possible, as early as possible. This may mean carrying more debt in the interest of creating a stable balance sheet where a person chooses to have debt, but also has the ability to eliminate that debt if needed.

Understanding that carrying debt in order to build wealth is ok does not mean that there are not lessons to be learned from your parents and grandparent's advice, however. What is important to understand from the Baby Boomer and Pre-Boomer Generations is that it is okay to borrow in order to build wealth and earn an income, as long as you do so in a safe and secure manner. It is also important to note that the right financial strategy must be implemented for the right personality type. (We will cover personality types in Chapter 5).

While borrowing strategies that pay off your mortgage slower may be beneficial to build wealth, borrowing to purchase consumer goods like cars, clothing, or anything that decreases rapidly in value is not. It is this type of borrowing to consume that has misled previous generations to believe that all debt is bad; this limiting belief has cost many people millions of dollars over their lifetime.

The Depression

Understanding where the pay off your mortgage mentality originated is an important first step to understanding your own personal financial decisions. A discussion of the farmer's homestead mentality only covers the origins of the ideology, so, to understand why this traditional wisdom has been passed on so feverishly, you must examine the factors that reinforced this ideology, namely the Great Depression.

Those who lived through the Great Depression saw 25% unemployment rates and an approximate 50% delinquency rate on mortgages (note that this is not the foreclosure rate, it is a measure of the amount of mortgages where payments were missed on at least one occasion). Men traveled on boxcars looking for work so that they could send money back to their families for food and clothing. It was grim, tough, and the most trying time in terms of finances in the last 100 years. Together, these hardships generated and promoted the fear of losing one's home to the bank and, even worse, not having enough money to put food on the table. A generation of proud North Americans put pride aside, stood in food lines, and accepted charity in order to survive.

The years prior to the Great Depression, the Roaring Twenties, were a time of prosperity. The economy was good, incomes were on the rise, and consumers borrowed money at extremely low interest rates in order to buy automobiles and other consumer goods. Companies borrowed money at similar rates for capital investments, leading to increased production and increased profits. The increase in spending had its upside, but it was not sustainable.

When the economy slowed, people cut spending and businesses cut jobs, and people found themselves out of work. Those who had little savings to speak of defaulted on loans and mortgages.

One may be quick to assume that the primary reason people were unable to repay loans was because of loose lending practices. On the contrary, most loans were granted to those who would be very likely to pay the money back: people who at the time the loans were made had secure jobs and more than enough income to qualify. However, it was the drastic and uncontrollable changes in the economy that caused many to go from having incomes that could cover their debt obligations to being unemployed and having no means of making their payments. Unemployment combined with a lack of savings made loan defaults inevitable. People were unprepared for an unexpected rainy day, so to speak.

Many believed that a person who had paid down their mortgage faster, but not in its entirety, during this time would have faired better than those who had made no efforts to pay down their mortgages at all. What they didn't realize was that if people had paid off a substantial amount, but not their entire mortgages, they would have still owed money on their homes at the exact same terms as they had borrowed it. This meant that they had the exact same monthly payments to make, even though they had paid off more of their mortgage, unless they refinanced to a longer term. Unfortunately, the economic circumstances of the depression would have made refinancing difficult because people who are unemployed have a difficult time qualifying for mortgages, even if they have a lot of equity in their property.

Interestingly, if you were someone who had paid off more of your mortgage than your neighbor, the increased amount of equity in your home, due to advanced payments, would have made your home more attractive for the banks to foreclose on. When a property has a smaller percentage owing, it has more equity and, thus, more upside potential for the bank. Even though you had been the better client who paid down your debt faster, you would have been the client with the biggest target on your back.

Short of being able to pay off all of your debt, paying down your mortgage would not have been the solution to your problems. The solution would have involved having the foresight to put away enough savings to weather the storm. The first and most obvious way of doing this would have been to put aside a percentage of your income every month into a "rainy day fund." This would have been a good idea to start. However, it alone would have been a slow way of saving money in order to be safe from creditors.

The second strategy would have required a bit more foresight and perhaps a little bit of creative thinking, but it would definitely have been more effective. The second strategy would have been to create a borrowing strategy, which didn't necessarily pay good debt off faster, but it would have allowed you to put more money into savings and investments. The idea would have been to lower the amount of money being used to pay off low interest secured debt, in order to increase the amount of money being put towards earning higher rates of return in safe investments. Putting money aside to grow, rather than pay it back into the mortgage, would ensure that you wouldn't have to worry about being able to make your monthly payments, because you would always have additional funds available in liquid investments. It would also ensure that you didn't have to leave the home where your son took his first steps and where you hosted your first holiday meal that went off without a hitch. Despite the fact that you would be increasing the amortization to lower your payments and paying more in interest over the life of your mortgage, you would be putting more money aside as early as possible to allow it to compound, which would ensure that you would always have enough money put aside to make your mortgage payments and put food on the table. You will see how to implement this kind of strategy and how it works in Chapter 7 when we discuss amortization arbitrage.

When discussing financial strategies, it is easy to forget that these strategies are not just about moving money around and keeping a roof over your head. These strategies are directly tied to your being – to your home – which is more than four walls and a roof. Your home is the place that contains your memories, the pencil markings on the wall marking your daughter's growth over the years, the place where you found out your wife was pregnant, and the place where you buried your dog beneath the apple tree. Regardless of the historical timeline, the importance of the family home has always been the same.

The Great Depression had a phenomenal impact on the North American psyche when it comes to money. But, what if things had been different? What if prior to The Great Depression, people borrowed to conserve rather than to buy the latest and greatest automobiles or the latest pieces of fashion? Would it have really made a difference if the majority of that era had the liquid assets put aside to pay monthly debt obligations for five to ten years, regardless of what the economy looked like? My hypothesis is yes.

Unfortunately, that was not what happened. Yes, a select few had the foresight to borrow in such a way that it made investing easier, but most did not. The adverse affects were that individuals who were once willing to embrace debt began to fear debt, and they spread this message of apprehension.

The ease of borrowing in the pre-depression era led many people to lose their material goods and their homes. The gradual acceptance of borrowing money to buy things that were wanted, rather than things that were needed, and the subsequent change in the majority of people's circumstances caused widespread fear. Never before had people borrowed so much, not realizing that it was possible for the economy to go sour and the means of paying for debt lost. This fear of debt, which was caused by purchases of material goods that declined in value once bought, caused the general opinion that debt was bad; this reinforced the farmer advice to pay off one's mortgage. "Debt to consume is bad" became "all debt is bad." The belief that all debt is bad could not be further from the truth.

Putting It All Together

What we all need to understand is that society has a tendency to believe and promote ideas not because they necessarily have merit, but because they are the easiest to believe. When majorities of people have faith in an idea, it makes it very hard to go against the grain. It also makes it very easy to just accept the opinion of the masses as fact. It is the "if so many people think its right, it must be right" mentality.

This is why the majority of people believe that the best financial strategy is to pay off all debt including your mortgage. They have been mystified by the masses that have told them to do so, just as the religious leaders of Galileo's time were and just as I was when challenged by my client.

Pay off your mortgage was great advice for the farmer, but it was only good advice for those who did not earn a living from their property. Furthermore, fear from the Great Depression reinforced this advice, not because it was the best advice, but because it was the advice that intuitively made the most sense given the situation of the day. Today, fear has lead to a misunderstanding of debt.

The easy attainability of high interest credit cards, along with the desire to have the latest gadgets, gizmos, and designer fashions, has led many to the opinion that all debt is bad. The fear of running up thousands of dollars in debt on goods that were merely consumable, not conservable, has created fear in taking on manageable debt in order to conserve. It has scared millions from owning a home and borrowing to build wealth. Worst of all, it has created ignorance among many with respect to the vast potential each and every one of us has to become truly wealthy.

The type of debt used to buy shoes, TVs, boats, or any other good that depreciates in value immediately after it has been purchased is bad debt. This is the kind of debt that can lead to financial hardships among those who let this type of borrowing go unchecked. Good debt is the type of debt used to buy homes and increase investments or other assets that over time will appreciate in value and, ultimately, lead to wealth. Good debt is the type of debt that you want to have because it will help you build wealth rapidly. This book will show you how to take advantage of this type of profitable debt.

2

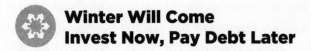

Winter Will Come
Invest Now, Pay Debt Later

Aesop's Fable

In a field one summer's day, a Grasshopper was hopping about, chirping and singing to its heart's content. An Ant passed by, bearing along with great toil an ear of corn he was taking to the nest.

"Why not come and chat with me," said the Grasshopper, "instead of toiling and moiling in that way?"

"I am helping to lay up food for the winter," said the Ant, "and I recommend that you do the same."

"Why bother about winter?" said the Grasshopper. "We have plenty of food at present."

But the Ant went on its way and continued its toil. When the winter came, the Grasshopper had no food, and it found itself dying of hunger, while it saw the ants distributing every day corn and grain from the stores they had collected in the summer. Then the Grasshopper knew:

"It is best to prepare for the days of necessity."[1]

---

1   Æsop. Fables, retold by Joseph Jacobs. Vol. XVII, Part 1. The Harvard Classics. New York: P.F. Collier & Son, 1909–14

* * *

Aesop's fable The Ant and the Grasshopper is a story that has been told for hundreds of years. The fable speaks of two characters: the Ant and the Grasshopper. The Ant spends his summer collecting food, creating a shelter and preparing for winter. The Grasshopper spends his time consuming food and does not worry about the winter months ahead until it is too late. Various versions of this tale have different endings; in all of them, the Grasshopper either dies or is forced to ask the Ant for help. What always remains the same in this fable is that the Ant's foresight and hard work lead to prosperity, and the Grasshopper suffers a less desirable fate.

Aesop's famous story reveals the benefits of hard work and planning over idleness. This same story also lends itself well to explaining the credit crisis of the last several years.

Since the turn of the millennium, homeowners in North America have seen dramatic increases in housing prices, followed by equally dramatic declines. Across both the United States and Canada (although more prevalent in the US), the rapid increase in housing prices led to an equally rapid increase in home equity for homeowners. For some, this increase in home equity has remained; for others, it has completely disappeared with the rapid deflation in housing prices. For those individuals who used their home equity as a bank account to consume—rather than to save—the consequences have been dreadful.

Much like the ill-fated Grasshopper that consumed all summer long, many North Americans withdrew money from their homes by refinancing their mortgages in order to spend. Many of these people bought cars, went on vacations, and renovated their homes with the money that they borrowed against their houses, spending as if housing inflation would last forever.

Unfortunately, just as the fable's winter was sure to come, so was the cold chill of a decrease in housing prices. Those who used their home equity like a bank account found themselves unable to eat or survive the downturn. On February 25, 2009, Oprah Winfrey profiled Sacramento, California, tent cities filled with homeless and jobless middle class workers who lost their homes overnight. Likened to third world refugee camps, residents spoke in tears of the inability to make rent or mortgage payments due to loss of jobs and lack of savings. Contrary to the popular belief that real estate values only go up, an entire continent quickly realized that real estate, much like the stock market and the economy as a whole, is cyclical—just as surely as a boom existed, a bust followed.

The Grasshoppers of our economy assumed that since the food was plentiful today it would stay plentiful tomorrow, and they spent the equity that they had garnered. Some acted like the Ant of Aesop's fable. These people saw the rise in housing prices much like the growing season of the summer months. They saw the opportunity not only to prepare for the coming winter months, but also for future seasons. They saw the growing season as a time to harvest and store in preparation for the long winter months ahead. The Ants were those who, instead of borrowing to consume, borrowed with investing and saving in mind.

Rebalancing the Portfolio

Imagine that in front of you is your new home—well groomed lawn, cultured stone façade, and sparkling clean windows—your 1800 square feet of debt. You hear your father's advice as you walk up the driveway, "Pay off your mortgage as fast as you can." You have heard him utter this advice countless times before; is this well-intentioned advice the best advice for your financial future? It does hold some merit. However, you may want to think twice about paying off your 1800 square feet in the shortest time possible.

Over the last several years, I have noticed a common trend among clients buying or refinancing homes. The trend has been a tendency to have more equity in their homes than invested or saved. In many cases, clients have little to no money in their savings yet have hundreds of thousands of dollars in their home equity. In other cases, people who have minimal savings have bought properties with little to no equity, exposing them to the risks associated with owning a home, while leaving them unprepared financially should something go wrong. Even for those who do have large amounts of equity, the lack of savings and investments carried by most people is alarming.

Many people argue that a person who has substantial equity in a property need not worry about having liquid assets, as they can always refinance or take out a second mortgage in order to release the equity locked into their house. This may be the true in some cases; however, it can also be a dangerous assumption. In the event of job loss or other financial difficulty, lenders are often hesitant to lend money, and when they do so, interest rates can be expensive and put homeowners at even greater risk of losing their homes.

It is important for homeowners to ensure that they have a substantial portion of their net worth available to them in the form of liquid assets. Liquid assets are the type of assets that can be sold or converted to cash easily and quickly. An example of liquid assets would be stocks, mutual funds, and short-term investment certificates. These types of assets can be sold and converted to cash within days if necessary, unlike real estate that can take months to sell or refinance. The ability to quickly access cash can be the difference between saving a home in a pinch and losing it to the bank.

Consider what would happen if a young couple heeded their father's advice to pay down their mortgage as quickly as possible, using all of their additional money to pre-pay their mortgage. Assume that after several years they found themselves in a recession like the one that happened around the Great Depression. For the several years prior to the recession, this couple would have put every penny left over at the end of the month towards paying down their principal, shortening the amortization of their mortgage drastically. Consider that the couple had paid nearly $30,000 extra into their mortgage, feeling as though they would make their parents proud. Unfortunately, because of the poor economy they found themselves in a position where they both lost their jobs. You would think that the $30,000 should be available to them; however, because they both lost their jobs, the bank was unwilling to let them re-borrow the funds. (Some banks do allow this if you have made all of your previous payments on time.)

Since every penny they had earned had been put towards the mortgage, they had little more than their last month's paycheques in their bank account, leaving them with few options except to go into foreclosure, sell, or find a lender that was willing to lend them the extra money they needed to survive, likely at an extremely high interest rate.

In this case, would it have been better for them to pay the mortgage down in the manner in which they did, or put the money aside into savings, investments, or, at worst, a rainy day fund? The obvious answer is the latter.

It becomes clear that paying off their mortgage should not have been the first priority, as doing so created a personal liquidity crisis. Their first priority should have been to make sure that a percentage of their net worth was readily available to them should they run into an emergency. The extra $30,000 they had paid in principal would have been more beneficial to them if invested or put it into a savings account. This amount of money would have given them at least six months to find a new job and get back on track.

Now, let's assume that the couple were in a position where they were able to qualify to re-borrow their $30,000 because a parent or family member was willing to cosign for them. What would happen if property values were declining? Much like in the previous scenario, the bank would be unwilling to lend the client the money, because the principal that they had paid into the mortgage was no longer supported by the value of the house. Their $30,000 had vanished because they had paid it into their mortgage.

Once again, it would have been more beneficial to put the money into some form of savings or investment account, just in case it was needed. Just like the Ant who stored food for the winter, it is important for a homeowner, or anyone else for that matter, to set aside money for a rainy day first and foremost before paying off low interest debt like a mortgage.

Saving for a rainy day is not the only reason to avoid paying off your mortgage at the expense of saving. Every dollar that you pay towards your mortgage or increasing your home equity can represent a potential opportunity cost. For example, if you were to receive a $10,000 bonus from work and you applied the bonus to pay off your mortgage that had a real interest rate of 6%, you would potentially be losing out on the opportunity to invest that money at a higher rate of return.

If you could invest that same money at a rate of 8%, your opportunity cost would be 2%. In other words, for every $6 you save in interest, you would be giving up $8 in earnings, losing you $2 or 25% of your money's opportunity. In terms of a mortgage, for every $60,000 you save in interest, you will lose $80,000 in income, for a net loss of $20,000, by paying off your mortgage in advance of investing for your future. Furthermore, this example is in very simple terms; the actual opportunity to earn is substantially greater due to the fact that money actually grows faster than it saves. (We will discuss how money grows in more detail in the next chapter.)

People fail in finance when it comes to thinking of their mortgages in terms of their overall financial picture, because they get so caught up in paying off their mortgage as fast as possible that they forget to think about the alternative financial options.

How Much Is Your Equity Earning You?

The advice to pay off one's home at all costs as quickly as possible can be dangerous advice, because it discounts the importance of diversifying your net worth.

Financial experts often speak of portfolio diversification: the practice of investing money in multiple types of investments in hopes that if one loses value, the others will make up for any losses. The strategy of portfolio diversification avoids putting all your eggs in one basket. Yet, diversifying your portfolio falls short of diversifying your net worth, which is equally (if not more) important.

Think of diversifying your portfolio as planting several different vegetables in a garden. By planting multiple varieties, you are hedging against growing conditions that may favor one crop over another. One year, the tomatoes may grow better than the carrots; another year, the carrots may grow better than the potatoes; and yet another year, lettuce may be the staple crop. Diversifying your net worth would be the equivalent of

35

planting a second garden in another field, hedging against anything that might go wrong in the first garden like an infestation of bugs or a rabbit problem. Paying off your mortgage without savings or investments, on the other hand, would be the equivalent of planting a field full of wheat, without planting any other crops, and simply hoping for the best.

Furthermore, it is important to understand that there is only so much that you can grow in one garden. Planting more seeds than what a garden is capable of producing is a waste of seed. There is a common misconception when it comes to paying off your mortgage that the more equity you have in a property, the higher rate of return if housing prices increase. However, having more equity in your home has nothing to do with the returns or declines that are caused by fluctuations in the value of a house.

If a property is worth $400,000, it makes no difference whether you have a $400,000 mortgage or no mortgage at all, with respect to fluctuations in the value of your house. If the property value increases by 5% to $420,000, the return is $20,000 no matter what the mortgage is. Many people believe that the person who has no mortgage in this type of scenario is better off; however, this is not necessarily the case, since the fluctuations in value are independent of the mortgage amount.

It is true that the person with no mortgage or a smaller mortgage is paying less interest; however, it is important to note that this has to do with the costs of owning the property, not the returns from fluctuations in value. When discussing the increase in net worth for both of these people, the result would be the same: it increased by $20,000.

When housing prices move downwards, on the other hand, there can be a significant difference in net worth changes, based not on the changes in the real estate value, but on what someone is doing with their equity. Those who choose to carry mortgages, even though they have the ability to pay all or part of them off, have a distinct advantage if they separate their equity and have it work to increase their net worth, even when real estate values decline. Diversifying equity can be done by borrowing against the value of the property while investing the money borrowed at a higher rate of return than the interest cost. This can be considered a hedge against declining property values.

For example, let's assume that someone with a $400,000 home and no mortgage can borrow $300,000 at a rate of 6%. Like in the previous example, we will also assume that they can earn 8% returns on the money that they invest. (We will assume that 6% is the true cost of borrowing, and 8% is the real rate of return). Every year, it would cost the client $18,000 in interest to borrow the money, but they would make $24,000 in income for a net income of $6,000. If this person's house value were decreasing by 5% per year, they would be losing $20,000 a year in real estate value. However, by diversifying their equity, they would only be losing $14,000 in personal net worth, fairing much better than if they had no mortgage at all. Furthermore, if the value of the house were to drop below $300,000, the client would reap the benefits of having equity that would otherwise have been lost on paper. One might argue that this strategy is dangerous and that there is a chance that the investments could lose a large amount of their value as well. This is true; however, the point of this example is not to argue the merits of different types of investments but, instead, to argue the merits of diversifying. One's investment strategies must align with what they believe is the safest and most effective use of their money.

The net worth increase effects of diversifying equity works

the same way if housing prices were increasing. If your equity is sitting idle in your home, it is subject to fluctuations in the real estate market; if it is being used to earn income, on the other hand, it can be a very effective tool not only in hedging against decreases in home values but also in creating wealth, assuming it is done in an effective and safe manner. By having more than a net worth that is comprised solely of home equity, one is able to ride out fluctuations in the housing market and in their other investments. Over the long term, diversifying will result in a group of assets that has risen in value over time, accelerating wealth creation, as opposed to just savings in mortgage interest. In the long term, an individual or couple should be able to pay off any mortgages used to invest, whenever they choose, rendering them mortgage free and with substantially more net worth than had they merely focused on paying off their mortgage.

The Ant and the Grasshopper fable serves as a great metaphor for the diversification of net worth. Like the Grasshopper, you should not take the present for granted. Increases in home value should not be seen as an opportunity to take advantage of temporary abundance. You should not consider increases in property values as an opportunity to spend recklessly. Just because money is plentiful today does not mean it will be tomorrow.

You must prepare for the future by making sure that you have savings and investments. You must have your net worth diversified not only in your investments but also in your overall financial picture. Not all of your personal net worth should be found in the equity of your home or solely in your investments, for that matter. There must be balance.

Like the Ant, you must also seize the opportunity to make sound financial decisions so that opportunity is not lost.

Through a strategy of net worth diversification, you can prepare like the Ant, while the Grasshoppers around you are left to struggle.

3

Paying Off Debt
How Much Does it Cost?

Imagine that it's the morning of your 65th birthday. You wake up with the excitement that you are another year older and more experienced and with the anticipation of celebrating your special day with your close family and friends. Yet, as you begin your morning routine—drinking a cup of coffee, reading the newspaper, and tidying the house—you are overcome with another feeling. It is a sensation that tickles in the bottom of your stomach: nervousness.

You push this feeling aside, since you have a few errands to run. After getting the oil changed in your car and picking up a package at the post office, you visit the office of your financial planner.

As you enter the office, you are again filled with that same sense of nervousness. After all, by general social standards, this is not just another birthday; you are not simply another year older. This is the day you were expected to retire.

You've done everything that you were supposed to do. As you sink into the comfortable leather chair, facing your investment guru, you consider everything you have done leading up to retirement. You've paid off your mortgage as fast as possible,

41

just like your father had instructed you to do the day that you moved into your first house. You have saved money where you could, being careful not to spend on luxuries that you could not afford, and you have invested intelligently. You place your hands on the smooth desktop and wait, wondering just what the outcome of all your hard work will be.

Your planner is, as always, straight to business. He explains that you have paid down your mortgage, amassed several hundred thousand dollars in a retirement fund, and owe very little. However, your planner informs you that in order to continue enjoying the lifestyle that you have become accustomed, you will likely have to continue working for several more years.

"How can this be?" you ask, feeling that nervousness rise up in your throat.

Your planner looks you straight in the eyes and responds, "If I had just been able to teach you a few simple concepts about money thirty to forty years ago, your current situation would be much different."

"How much different?" you ask.

"A few million dollars different," he replies, "but there is still hope for you. I have a few more tricks that I can teach you."

"Please explain."

"Well, let's start with what you should have done and why, and then we can get to what you need to do now."

"But, the past is the past," you respond hoping that your planner does not make you feel worse than you already do. "How is what I should have done going to make any difference?"

"There are two reasons that it is important to discuss what you should have done. The first reason is that in order to understand where you need to go, it is important that you understand what has and hasn't worked for you in the past. The second reason is that if I can teach you what you should have done, it gives you the opportunity to pass the knowledge on, especially to those you care about so that others don't make the same mistakes."

You begin to realize that even though you had done all of the right things in the past—at least what you thought were the right things—there is still so much more to learn. You begin to feel open to the new concepts that are about to be explained for the sake of your financial future.

You lean in, ready to listen as your financial planner begins to explain some simple concepts that you must know about how money grows and how important it is to take control of your financial education.

How Money Grows

One of the most detrimental fallacies in finance is that there is plenty of time to save money. This is not the case. To save and invest should be taught to every child the day that they earn their first dollar. Furthermore, children should also be shown how money grows as early as possible as well.

Helping a child, or an adult for that matter, understand how money grows can be done through a simple analogy. Imagine having to push a parked pickup truck down the street. At first, you would barely be able to move it. The truck would be heavy, and it would move very little. However, as the truck begins to move it become much easier to push, until eventually, it almost moves on its own. As it gets to the point where you are running and pushing as fast as you can and the only thing stopping you from pushing the truck any faster is the fact that you physically cannot move any quicker, you reach the top of a hill. As the truck reaches the crest, gravity begins to pull it faster and faster towards the bottom, leaving you standing at the top of the hill no longer exerting any effort at all. Momentum has taken over. When money grows, it works in a very similar way: lots of effort up front and very little later on.

Saving and investing early is the financial equivalent of getting the truck moving. You exert the initial force that allows saving to become easier and easier. As you save more, the momentum eventually takes over, to the point where your money grows at a rate that will create effortless wealth. However, much like getting the truck moving is not an easy task, developing the habits and discipline to continually save is the hardest part. If at any point you decide to give up, you have to start the tough part all over again. Furthermore, every time you stop, you have a little less energy, which reduces your ultimate potential.

There are many other ways to show an adult or child how money grows. One of my favorite methods was my mother's method of choice. She set up a simple investment account for me and let me keep track of the results.

My mother was brilliant in this matter. She started by setting up an account and taking me through an investor analysis that determined what my risk tolerances were. With some guidance, we were able to determine that I was a not averse to risk, and I was a long-term investor interested in growth. Based on this analysis, she was able to help me pick an investment portfolio (not pick one for me). The portfolio consisted mostly of dividend funds and equity funds with a small percentage in bonds. Every month, she would show me the statements and discuss with me how my investments were doing. After several years, she was able to show me how my money had grown far beyond my expectations, even though I hadn't noticed much of a change on a month to month basis. For a child, this method was beyond effective; it was life altering.

However, when teaching adults how money grows, one might not have several years to set up a sample account, so another way to show someone how money grows is through examples, such as the following:

If you had $100 that was growing at a rate of 10% per year, the value after one year would be $110 ($100 + 10% or $10). After 2 years it would be $121 ($110 + 10% or $11), and after three years it would be worth $133.10 ($121 + 10% or $12.10). After three years, your $100 is worth $133.10. This means that if you had failed to save and invest $100 in the first year, you would need to save and invest $133.10 in the third year to be in the same net position. Your $100 today is in effect worth $133.10 three years from now. This doesn't seem like a big deal on $100, but to put it in perspective, if you were to perform the same calculation on $10,000 that you could have saved and invested now instead of 3 years from now, you would need to come up with an extra $3,331 to be in the same net position! While $33.10 is an easy amount of money to save, $3,331 is not quite as easy to accumulate. If you waited three years to save $10,000, you would be 33.1% behind.

If you had waited until year three to begin investing instead of investing in year one and had not made up the $3,331, 40 years later you would have $112,000 less. Waiting a mere three years to put $10,000 away would have hindered the exponential growth possible at a later date. In other words, waiting three years to save $10,000 at age 25 because you decided you wanted to upgrade your Civic or buy a motorcycle would cost you a Corvette or Mercedes at age 65.

The belief that two or three years isn't that big of a deal is shortsighted. In actuality, the way in which money grows would mean that you would lose substantially more than you think in the long run. In order to help understand the impor-

45

tance of early investing when I am talking with clients, I like to use one of my favorite examples from my first book, *Golf Balls Don't Float,* to illustrate.

Assume for a moment that you are a golfer, and a friend offers you the choice to compete against them in either a game for $100 a hole or 10 cents on the first hole, with the bet doubling on every hole. The first hole would be worth 10 cents, the second hole would be worth 20 cents, the third hole would be worth 40 cents, and so on until the round was complete. Lets also assume that you know for a fact that you can beat your friend. Not only are you sure that you can beat him but you can mop the floor with him. With the knowledge that a golf course has 18 holes, which competition would you choose in order to maximize your potential returns?

Most people would choose the first bet because playing for $100 a hole would equal potential winnings of $1800: a lot of money for a friendly game of golf. Yet, if your goal was to maximize your winnings, and you failed to select the 10-cent bet that doubled every hole, you would have lost out on quite a bit of potential earnings. Here is why:

The first hole is worth 10 cents.

The second is worth 20 cents.

The third is worth 40 cents.

The fourth is worth 80 cents.

The fifth is worth $1.60.

The sixth is worth $3.20.

The seventh is worth $6.40.

The eighth is worth $12.80.

The ninth hole is worth $25.60, just enough to cover the meal at the end of the round. Even if you had won every single hole at this point, you would only have won $51.10, which is just half of what you could have won on one hole with the first bet.

Here is where things start to get interesting; the tenth hole is worth $51.20.

The eleventh is worth $102.40. At this point you have just reached the level that one hole would have made you on the first bet.

The twelfth hole is worth $204.80.

The thirteenth is worth $409.60.

The fourteenth is worth $819.20.

The fifteenth is worth $1,638.40. You are now probably coming to realize that, the $100 bet had the least profit potential.

The sixteenth hole is worth $3,276.80.

The seventeenth is worth $6,553.60.

The eighteenth is worth an astonishing $13,107.20.

The total potential profit for the round is $26,214.30, which is much more money than that of the $100 per hole bet. There are actually three individual holes where you could win more than the entire amount of the other bet, and one more hole that is very close. The assumption that there was no way that a bet that started at 10 cents could possibly be worth more than that of a $100-a-hole bet could have been a costly decision. Yet, off the golf course, people make the same types of assumptions with their money everyday.

The reality is this: if you had decided to wait until the fourth hole to start your bet, the potential outcome of your bet would have been $22,937.60 less. Those first few holes drastically impact the value of the bet because, like in the example of the truck, the bet needs that extra time at the beginning in order to get the momentum rolling to its full potential. Saving and investing work the same way. The earlier you start, the bigger the impact at the end. In fact, you are better off starting early in small amounts than you are finishing late and saving large amounts.

The point here is simple: saving as much money as possible early is the most important decision that you can make when it comes to creating financial freedom. Not doing so will require you to work twice as hard if not harder to save the same amount of money if you wait even just a small period of time.

Savings vs. Growth

In addition to common misconceptions about how money grows, there is one other misconception about how money works that I see everyday in my mortgage business. That misconception is that money used to pay down your mortgage saves you the same amount of money as it would earn you, assuming that your rate of return and mortgage rate were equal. The fact of the matter is that money will always grow faster than it saves because money that is growing experiences exponential returns, where money used to pay down debt experiences diminishing returns. In other words, when money grows, you earn interest on your interest. When money is used to pay off debt, you are saving less interest with every period that passes.

For example, $10,000 paid into a 25-year mortgage at 5% would save you $7,488. That same $10,000 at an annual rate of return of 5% over 25 years would become $33,863, for a return of $23,863. Thus, when a client asks me whether they should pay down their mortgage or invest the money, I almost always tell the client to invest. The difference between the return on investing and the savings is what is known as the opportunity cost. Those who believe that paying off their mortgage as fast as possible is the best use of their money are often unaware of the opportunity cost associated with paying down their mortgage in advance.

There are cases where I don't tell clients to invest first, however. These cases involve circumstances where the client is deemed highly likely to spend any money saved, or when from a numbers standpoint, it doesn't make sense. An example of this type of circumstance would be when the client has high interest rate debt. Obviously, it is important to run the numbers to determine where money can be most efficiently used to either save or earn. When money can save more than it can earn, then debt pay down should be the priority. However, when it can earn more than it can save, investing should take precedence. The key to furthering your financial freedom is to understand all of the options and to choose the most financially beneficial opportunities. If you find this difficult to do on your own there are a variety of experts who can help you.

The Mortgaged Millionaire

4

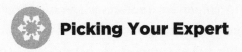

Picking Your Expert

Darcy Reynolds is a survivor. In an industry where big box stores such as Golf Town and Nevada Bob's have taken over, Reynolds continues to thrive, where few other independent golf stores have made it.

Reynolds is the owner of Golf Plus +, one of Calgary's oldest and most established golf shops. His store is clean, well designed, and fully stocked with equipment from top golf manufacturers. Golf Plus +'s clientele ranges from beginner golfers to some of Alberta's top amateurs, and surprisingly, a large number of his clients are golfers who belong to private golf courses. This may seem unusual, as golfers who hold memberships at private clubs are typically loyal to their club's pro shop, but Reynolds has been able to break this practice.

Reynolds has acquired a customer base that would normally seek advice from their golf pro, and he has managed to stay afloat despite mass advertising and the price cutting of his large competitors. Where other independents have failed, Reynolds has been able to grow his business and survive in a hostile marketplace. One may think that his ability to survive has been due to an innovative marketing strategy or through competitive pricing. While these things have had an impact, the real reason for Reynolds' success has more to do with his perceived role as an advisor instead of as a salesperson.

Big box stores and high-pressure sales seem to be synonymous in the golf industry. Among the racks of golf clubs, bags, and clothing, there are a small army of commissioned salespeople or hourly employees. In stores where salespeople earn commission, there is a strong incentive to first sell products that carry a higher rate of commission, before selling products that may be more beneficial to the customer. Stores where commission is paid often draw the best talent, but these may not always be the people who are most concerned with making sure every client is absolutely satisfied with their purchase. Stores that pay on a salary or hourly only basis, on the other hand, have their own issues that include, but are not limited to, laziness, lack of attention to the customer, and low levels of expertise. Employees who work in a fixed income scenario have a different set of incentives, which usually involves optimizing their effort to work ratio. In most cases, they do not care what they sell or to whom; they are more interested in doing the minimum amount of work in order to feel satisfied in their job at their given pay rate. Stores with this type of remuneration system often have employees who are more interested in their conversations with coworkers and other distractions than helping the customer; this is in contrast of course to the over aggressive nature of commissioned employees. In either scenario, customers of big box stores are often more likely to purchase the wrong product, either because of lack of proper advice or pressure to buy a product that carries a higher commission rate.

In contrast, at Golf Plus +, Reynolds understands a concept that few other golf equipment salespeople acknowledge: selling golf clubs and building a business is about having a passion for golf and the client's best interest. Reynolds is the trusted advisor of his clients. He goes out of his way to make sure that his customers purchase the products best suited to them and that they are custom fit (a process which takes a minimum of 30 minutes and is the equivalent of taking a normal shoe and building a custom orthotic). Reynolds will even go one step further. He orders the products he sells custom fit from the manufacturer, ensuring that the warranty is not void, all while picking up the extra costs associated with specially ordered clubs. Furthermore, Reynolds remembers nearly every client's name, even after only one meeting. The end result is a sense of trust that keeps Golf Plus +'s clients returning year after year. Reynolds has become the golf advisor of thousands of golfers in the Calgary area—a label usually reserved for local club pros. Reynolds' role as a trusted advisor is the reason why his store has thrived amidst a storm of big box retailers and green grass pro shops.

The Problem with Banks

As discussed previously, Reynolds has established and built his business by being the trusted advisor to the golfers who buy from him. A customer can walk into his store, talk about any issues with their game, and receive sound advice on what to do to fix the problems. If the problem can be solved by selling the customer a new piece of equipment, then Reynolds will sell the client a club. If it can be solved by changing his swing slightly or through other means, then he is glad to help free of charge. Clients know that they can look to Reynolds for help, that he will always be objective in his advice, and that he already has knowledge of the client's golf game. Furthermore, clients recognize that Reynolds is in business to make a profit, but he will not compromise his business by trying to make an extra buck

53

or two. These are the characteristics that a client looks for when they are seeking an advisor, and this is what Reynolds delivers: service that his big box competitors cannot deliver.

Banks tend to have similar customer service to big box stores. Typical bank employees are motivated in much the same way as the employees at the large chain stores that litter the big city landscape. The most talented employees are typically commissioned or heavily compensated based on performance, and they act aggressively in order to earn maximum compensation. Salaried employees, on the other hand, tend to show indifference towards their client's and are usually more concerned with putting in their hours than making sure every client is completely satisfied with their current banking scenario. Of course, there are exceptions to the rule. The exceptions are typically those who care deeply about their clients and their financial success—much like how Reynolds cares deeply about his clients.

My mother, who has been with the same branch at BMO Bank of Montreal for eight years and with BMO for a total of 40 years, is one of these exceptions. Much like Darcy Reynolds, she is the trusted advisor to her long-term clients—many of whom have followed her from branch to branch as changes in her job brought new opportunities.

In contrast to my mother, it is uncommon to find an employee in a bank who stays in the same job, in the same location, for more than a couple of years at a time. Employees in these institutions are constantly looking to move higher in the ranks in order to earn more pay for the hours they work or bigger job titles and more responsibility. If not given the opportunity to excel within the organization, they will often move to an institution that will offer greater opportunities. A common occurrence in the banking industry is for an employee to be more valuable to the competition than they are to the bank that they currently work for. Oddly enough, banks tend to treat their clients in the same way.

For those who have very strong relationships with their trusted financial advisors, this tendency to move may not be a big issue as their relationship with the advisor will allow them to follow that advisor to a new branch or institution. For the average customer, on the other hand, it is likely that the representative that initially arranged their mortgage or investments will not be the same person they meet with five years down the road when their mortgage comes up for renewal or their portfolio needs to be overhauled. As a result, it becomes very hard to establish an advisor-advisee relationship.

In an environment where your banker is always changing, it is difficult to know for sure if your bank actually understands your needs and is placing you in the products that suit you best. Uncertainty in a client's banking relationship makes a customer more vulnerable to the aggressive commissioned salespeople who are actually most interested in their paycheque.

Banks have one other major problem, which is that they only provide one suite of products. You can't get RBC products at Scotia Bank, and you can't get TD Canada Trust products at BMO. Furthermore, it is rare that one institution's FSM would be familiar with the products of other institutions. Which leads to this question: how do you know that you are getting the product best suited for you, if you only visit one bank? The short answer is that you don't, unless you have a trusted advisor aware of products offered by all institutions and who is not limited in their ability to discuss them because of the logo on their business card. The only way to find someone who is aware of products offered at multiple institutions is to deal with independent mortgage brokers or financial planners, who, by the way, are likely to be commissioned, aggressive, and more concerned with their needs than their clients'.

The Problems with Mortgage Brokers

It is apparent that there are some drawbacks to going directly to your bank to get your mortgage and investment advice. Banks have a limited product line, a lack of personal relationships, potentially high staff turnover, and a limited knowledge of products available through the competition. There are also some advantages. When dealing with a bank, you are less likely to have to deal with a commission salesperson (although mortgage specialists and some investment advisors are commissioned and highly aggressive). There is also the advantage of only having to deal with one company for all of your financial needs, which can entitle you to discounts and better service if you have enough business with a particular bank. However, is that really enough to convince someone to deal with one bank exclusively? My opinion is no.

When it comes to your mortgage, there are definite advantages to using a mortgage broker, although there are some fallacies that need to be addressed. The first fallacy is the belief that mortgage brokers will always get you the best rate. To try to lead you to believe that the five major banks are not pricing leaders and that they don't make their best rates available to their best clients is false. There are some occasions when a mortgage broker just can't get as good of a rate as your bank. In almost all cases though, this inability has more to do with a high wealth private banking relationship than it does with an average Joe walking through the front door of a bank and getting a great rate. Yes, it is possible to get a better rate directly from a bank than what a mortgage broker can offer you, but chances are that you aren't rich enough to get it.

Instead, what is more accurate is that mortgage brokers know which banks have the best rates at any given point in time, and they can potentially save you from having to negotiate with your bank for their best rate. This may mean that they know to go to Scotia Bank for the best five-year rate, but it does not mean that a client could not walk into a Scotia Bank on their own and get the same rate if they were a good client or a strong negotiator. In some instances, the best rate on the market is only available through a broker exclusive lender. In any event the mortgage broker will typically know where the best rates and products are, and will save you the trouble of having to seek this information yourself. Think of the mortgage broker in terms of an extremely informed friend.

The second issue with the belief that a mortgage broker will always get you the best rate is that some banks do not deal with mortgage brokers. A mortgage broker who tells their clients that they will always get the best rate is only doing so if they are willing to give up a client to a bank who they may not be able to deal with. Given the nature of a commission driven industry, giving up a client is unlikely. A more accurate statement with respect to rates is not that a mortgage broker will always get you the best rate, but that a good mortgage broker generally knows where to find the best rate. The guarantee that you will get that rate is another story.

Another fallacy about mortgage brokers is that they deal with 30, 40, 50, 60, or 70 lenders. It is not uncommon for brokers to try to tell their client that they have access to or deal with a high number of lenders. Currently, there are 77 lenders available on Filogix Expert, which is the system primarily used to submit mortgages by brokers in Canada. However, no mortgage broker will ever use all of these lenders. The truth is that most mortgage brokers deal with a maximum of 10 lenders per year, and the majority of their business only goes to two or three of them. In fact, having two or three lenders that are used primarily is better than having 77 that are used sparsely, mainly because the broker will get better service from lenders that they have formed a relationship with, and they will also, in many cases, get preferential rates.

Why, then, do brokers mislead clients with their statements about the number of lenders that they deal with and the rates they provide? The answer is simple: brokers need a way to differentiate themselves from the banks. They believe that the best way to do this is by advertising best rates and copious amounts of options, when, in fact, they merely have competitive rates and typically use only two or three different lenders. While this has been the norm for most mortgage brokers, it is the wrong way of differentiating. Instead, the appropriate method of differentiating would be to become a Darcy-Reynolds-type of advisor.

Picking the Right Person for the Job

If the two most common ways that mortgage brokers differentiate themselves are nothing more than exaggerations of the realities of the job, how should someone go about picking the right mortgage broker? To answer this question, we must examine the two inherent issues with the mortgage industry. The first issue is that there is little barrier to entry for a mortgage broker, and the second issue is that the industry is extremely sales oriented.

Depending on the Canadian province, licensing requirements can be anywhere from nothing to a 3-month course taken at a local community college. In most cases, the only previous level of education required is a high school diploma or equivalent, unlike stockbrokers or accountants for example, who are typically required to have, at minimum, a university degree.

Most students in the mortgage broker programs expect to make easy money while working minimal hours, which is indicative of a key problem with the industry: people don't take it seriously enough. In order to make decent money in the industry, a mortgage broker must work full time hours. There is no such thing as a part time broker who makes $100,000 a year. There is also no such thing as easy money. These fallacies have generated a large number of part time brokers who make dedicated professionals in the industry look bad due to their lack of knowledge and professionalism.

The second inherent issue is the hunt-and-kill mentality of the industry. Mortgage brokers are typically more concerned with where their next commission cheque is coming from, how much they are getting paid on a particular deal, and making sure that they are able to close it than they are with where their client will be several years down the road. This is not their fault, however; this mentality stems from being a commissioned salesperson. Commissioned sales people take the necessary action to get paid. When visiting an Audi dealership, the salesperson will always make an Audi out to be a superior car to a BMW. If that same salesperson moved to a BMW dealership, they would flip on you, leading you to believe that the BMW is the better car. In reality, they know that the two cars are pretty comparable, and which one is better comes down to personal preference. Their sales pitches change based on what the product is that they are selling and what will put the commission cheque in their pocket. This is what makes many mortgage brokers more like the commissioned salespeople who wander the floors of car dealerships and big box stores than their salaried counterparts.

What is a customer to do? Deal with the complacency of

the salaried bank employee, hoping that they are smart enough and stick around long enough to help the customer make the right decisions? Or should the customer take a chance on a commissioned mortgage broker and hope that they are more interested in putting the client in the right mortgage than collecting a commission cheque? The answer is that the customer needs to find his or her own Darcy Reynolds of mortgages. How do you do this? You begin by finding someone who you will always be available, someone who you can trust to give you objective advice, regardless of whether or not it makes them any money, and someone who has prior and continued knowledge of your situation.

The Mortgage Advisor

In the United States, there is a growing movement towards a concept known as mortgage planning (what much of this book is based on from a Canadian perspective). A Washington mortgage broker, Stephen Marshal is leading this movement.

Marshal and his colleagues have created an entire network as well as an accreditation process around the concept of assimilating mortgage planning with financial planning. This organization believes that the two concepts are not separate entities, and I would tend to agree.

In Canada, Mortgage Architects is leading the way in mortgage planning. Mortgage Architects has gone as far as branding all of their agents, associates, and partners as "Planners." This has led to many other mortgage associates working with other companies to adopt this title, though few understand the concept itself.

A mortgage planner assesses not only the mortgage needs of a client, but also addresses their overall financial needs. They will look at a client's risk tolerance, make suggestions as to asset allocation and financial strategy, and also refer clients to other financial professionals where needed. Furthermore, a mortgage planner will ensure that the client's mortgage needs compliment their insurance and financial planning needs. In many cases, mortgage brokers who call themselves planners isolate their planning solely to the client's mortgage, defeating the purpose of having a mortgage planner.

My own experiences in real estate are an example of why mortgage planning is important. When I bought my first condo, I put as much money down as I could possibly afford in order to save on mortgage insurance premiums. I also arranged the shortest amortization I could afford in order to pay my mortgage off as fast as possible, potentially saving me thousands of dollars in interest. My whole strategy was centered on paying as little interest as possible, which completely neglected the rest of my financial strategy. If you ask most mortgage brokers, who call themselves mortgage planners, to explain what mortgage planning is, they will tell you that mortgage planning is the process of making sure that you pay as little interest as possible; they could not be more wrong.

On the second condo I purchased, I took a completely different approach. I looked at the interest costs I would be paying on the mortgage, the cost of the insurance premium, and the benefits of a longer versus a shorter amortization. I also looked at the opportunity cost of a larger down payment, the returns I could expect by investing that money elsewhere, and what I could do with the additional money every month from having a longer amortization and subsequently a lower payment. (I will discuss all of these concepts in depth later.) I made several key, yet conservative, assumptions and ran several different models of what my net worth could potentially look like at the end of my mortgage, given the different scenarios. I

61

also took a serious look at which model I was most likely to feel comfortable with and be able to stick to long term.

Next, I made an educated choice based on my risk tolerances and my goals to put as little money down as possible over the longest amortization possible, investing the money I did not put down on the property immediately and contributing additional amounts to that investment monthly. My mortgage strategy and my financial strategy therefore became intertwined, making my mortgage decisions on my second property much sounder and more of a plan than a strategy. By examining all the options to build wealth, not necessarily just an interest saving solution, I was mortgage planning.

The difference between these two scenarios is subtle, yet in financial terms, it is substantial. The first mortgage decision I made was very mortgage specific. It looked solely at the mortgage and the interest costs, as well as the length of time I would have held the mortgage. I did not look at the opportunity cost of the money that I was immediately taking out of investments. It did not take into consideration that I was moving money out of an investment that was earning me more money than what reducing my mortgage was saving me.

The second mortgage decision, on the other hand, did take into consideration the opportunity costs of pulling money out of my investments and the cost of paying the mortgage down more quickly. This consideration allowed me to make a decision that over the life of the mortgage will not necessarily save me interest; in fact, it will cost me substantially more interest than if I had chosen the opposite. However, in the long run, my total net worth will be substantially higher, even given the higher interest costs. This is the type of decision that a mortgage planner assists their clients with.

Mortgage planners also need to go one step further. Many

so-called mortgage planners sell a "one strategy fits all" solution to their clients (such as the Smith Maneuver or TDMP). This practice of selling one strategy is financially reckless. The Smith Maneuver, for example, is a valid strategy, but it's not for everyone. In fact, this type of leveraged strategy can turn promises of rapid wealth building into an even quicker financial crisis, if set up for the wrong type of client. Mortgage planners therefore need to become quasi-financial counselors who help clients understand what type of financial personality type they are and how to build a strategy around that understanding.

A mortgage planner needs to be slightly more than just a planner; they need to become a trusted advisor. A mortgage planner needs to be someone who begins by understanding the client, helps the clients understand themselves, and assists in making financially sound, long-term decisions. If a mortgage planner can fulfill this role, then they are a Darcy-Reynolds-type of mortgage advisor.

In summary, a mortgage advisor would first and foremost care about their client's best interests. A client's best interests would come before all else, including collecting a commission cheque. The advisor would be informed on all mortgage products, available to them or not. They would put the client in the mortgage best suited to their individual financial needs, taking into consideration their complete financial picture and goals. If the client did not have a set of financial goals, the mortgage advisor would help establish them. If they knew of a better product at an institution that they were unable to deal with, they would release the client to that institution without hesitation, knowing that the client would return faithfully in the future, bringing with them a herd referrals. The Darcy-Reynolds-type of advisor would meet with the client regularly to reassess their mortgage needs. Furthermore, they would assist them in creating and implementing a mortgage strategy that would free them of their mortgage sooner than they ever thought possible.

5

Your Personality Sucks (Unless You Understand It)

The Five Cousins

In late July, my grandparents hosted family reunions in our backyard. At this time of year, the leaves were at their deepest shade of green, and the apples were always weighing down the branches of the trees alongside the fence. It was at this peak of summer that I anticipated the arrival of my extended family.

My grandparents, aunts, uncles, and all of my cousins would get together to share a meal and to share the stories that composed our lives in between visits. Some summers, distant cousins would drive in from Seattle and Vancouver, arriving at the small town on the eastern edge of Alberta, where our gatherings were held. These cousins would pack along with them their big city personalities.

It was always an exciting time for me. Even though we were all part of the same family, there were distinct differences in the beliefs and values among us. Such differences were apparent in everything from political debates, to parenting techniques, to the way each family treated their finances. These differences were even visible between the young members of the family; while we may have all enjoyed jumping on the trampoline and racing bicycles down the alleyway, we definitely diverged when it came to developing money management philosophies.

My grandfather would give each of his grandchildren two things when they came to visit. The first was the choice between a pack of Juicy Fruit or Doublemint gum. The second was money—anywhere from one to five dollars, depending on how generous he felt that year.

Upon receiving these gifts, each of the kids would proudly show their parents before going about the process of trying to figure out what to do with the money. It was interesting to watch the children in a very adolescent manner make financial decisions in the same way their parents would.

Some of the kids, who I like to call the Spenders, would immediately run to the convenience store and spend all of their money on candy. Each bag of candy carried one of two fates for those children; it would either render them sick by the end of the day or be taken away by their parents to prevent any impending stomachaches. Years later, the early childhood diagnosis of the Spenders would hold true for most of the children, as every penny earned in their adult years would be spent just as quickly on material goods. The difference in adulthood was spending with such indulgence caused more pain than just a stomachache.

I remember one cousin being praised for not running to the candy store like his cousins. His parents were always proud of him; he had been taught to save every penny. He would take whatever money he was given, stick it in his pocket, and then transfer it to a baby blue piggy bank with no openings, other than the slot in the back, as soon as he got home. Apparently, he was saving it for a rainy day or to buy something more worthwhile than candy. The interesting thing about him, though, was that he could never seem to part with the money once he had saved it. Every year, his parents would tell the entire family how proud they were of their son because he had gone the entire year without spending the money he had received the year before. The poor child would consistently see something in a store that he wanted, think about buying it, and almost always come to the conclusion that the pain of parting with the money he had saved was not worth whatever pleasure could be gained from spending it. He had a completely irrational fear of spending money, even though he had absolutely no experience spending. In hindsight, his parents' praise of his saving habit became more of a reinforcement of his fear to spend, and more than likely, his parents were also the cause of his spending fears. He was the consummate Saver of the family, and today, in his adult years, he owns a small house, has a small bank account, and not a whole lot to show for his savings because not only is he afraid to spend, but he is also equally afraid to invest any of his money. To this day he still saves every penny he earns.

On a particular late July reunion, one of my cousins brought a friend along. He was well read, always quoting from classic novels, and speaking of the biographies of musicians and actors. He knew the pH of lemonade and could tell you anything you ever wondered about the Paleozoic era. Even as a child, he practiced veganism to promote the ethical treatment of animals, and he was well researched to back up his conviction to a diet free of dairy and meat products. At less than 10 years old, this kid seemed to be a freak of nature. You could tell he was one of those individuals who did very well in school because he had a tendency to ask a lot of questions, including a one word question that especially annoyed one of my uncles: "why?"

Instead of spending his money, he spent most of the July day trying to figure out what to do with it. He couldn't decide

67

if he wanted to spend it on a vegan-friendly treat, place it in a coin machine that dispensed key chains, or simply keep the coins in his pocket. By the time he had finally come to a decision later that night, it was too late because all of the stores were closed. He didn't seem to mind though, as it gave him more time to think over his decision. The next morning, he began his whole analysis process again, just to make sure he knew exactly what he wanted. He spent the rest of his visit questioning his decision and ended up going home with the money. He was a Scrutinizer. He considered every last option so thoroughly that he was unable to make a decision at all.

The most memorable of the group were two distant cousins. These two were never interested in menial things like 5-cent candy; they were always interested in purchasing the biggest chocolate bars, ice cream cones, and toys that they could find. In many cases, they would have to go to their parents to borrow extra money to get what they wanted. Of course, once they had acquired their big-ticket purchase, they would parade it around as if they were in possession of an article of exclusivity. Needless to say, later in life, these are the two that have the hardest time with their finances. As adults, they live paycheck-to-paycheck, often spending more than what they make. As Strugglers, they are always willing to borrow a little extra, just as they did as kids, in order to buy more extravagant things that they really can't afford. They live mostly off credit, and they are constantly accumulating more and more debt.

The Odd Child Out

Long after my grandfather had passed away, I sat with my parents and my grandmother one Christmas eve, discussing how my grandfather was able to help the farmers in his community survive and how he had positioned himself to do so through saving and investing. As we talked, my grandmother began to tell me about the soft spot that I held in my grandfather's heart. She looked at me, taking my hand between her soft palms, and said, "He was always so impressed by how you handled your money, and you always got a little extra for that."

I was lucky; my mother was a saver by every definition of the word. My father, on the other hand, was an entrepreneur, who was always interested in how he could make an extra buck. He would buy and sell cars, develop basements, and do anything to turn nothing into something and something into more. At some point, I put two and two together. I became a hybrid of my mother's savings habits and my father's desire to have more. Even at an early age, I became what you could consider an investor. I realized that if I saved and found a way to make my money or my possessions grow in value, then I could spend like the spenders, and I would still be better off than the savers—all while building wealth and never having to worry like the scrutinizer or borrow like the struggler.

As a child, I put these characteristics into action, much to my grandfathers delight, by figuring out that the money and gum my grandfather had given us was more than just a gift: it was an opportunity. By trading and bargaining, I was able to turn small gifts into excess abundance.

My grandfather always kept a supply of two types of gum: Juicy Fruit and Doublemint. Each pack of gum was worth 75 cents, and there were 10 pieces of gum in the pack. This made each piece worth 7.5 cents. I also knew that Juicy Fruit was the gum favored by most of my cousins, so I always made sure to choose it over Doublemint gum, even though I preferred the minty flavor of Doublemint to the sweet fruity flavor of Juicy Fruit.

Given that each piece of gum was worth 7.5 cents, I could

trade one piece of gum for two or more of the five-cent candies my cousins typically bought, a ten-cent candy, or, if I was really lucky, a 25-cent candy, and I would be better off from a "net worth" perspective. The beauty of the five-cent candy was that when a cousin returned from the candy store with a huge bag of them, there would appear to be an abundance of candy in comparison to a meager 10-pack of gum. Most of my cousins never took the time to try to figure out what each piece of gum was worth. The other children typically did not buy more Juicy Fruit at the candy store because they were already in possession of it when they were making their purchases. When they returned home however, it was easy to point out how much candy they had in relation to gum, making the gum more valuable in their eyes. The change in perceived value would make it easy to convince them to trade some candy for some gum, at least until the candy was almost gone. They were irrational consumers.

The scarcity of candy that resulted from my cousins trading it to me and then eating the rest was exactly what I wanted. Gum would always last longer than the candy, because it was consumed one piece at a time and not immediately. Thus, there would always be a shift to an abundance of gum. A bag of thirty candies, on the other hand, could be gone in less than 15 minutes, assuming a parent hadn't snatched it away, leaving nothing but sticky fingers and a blue tongue behind. When the candy started to run out, I was left with the majority of the candy because I had traded for it earlier.

With all of their money spent and candy eaten, I had cornered the candy market. Since gum was still in abundance and candy was in short supply and high demand, it made the candy worth substantially more than its original value. I would trade back a five-cent candy for two or three pieces of 7.5-cent gum.

Eventually, I would end up with the original money that my grandfather had given me, a few pieces of candy for myself, and three or four packs of gum. In the course of a reunion day, I would usually more than quadruple my "net worth."

I also had one more trick up my sleeve. I knew that my grandfather favored Doublemint gum, the same gum that I liked, and that he always had extra in the giant bulk packages that he bought. All I had to do was be around whenever he decided to have a piece, and I would be offered a piece as well. Unlike the other kids who would turn their noses up at a piece of Doublemint gum, I rarely had to dip into the stash I had created for myself, allowing me to take it home and enjoy it there. My cousins went home empty handed. Furthermore, my grandfather was always willing to trade back the packs of Juicy Fruit that I had acquired for Doublemint, because it allowed him to save the Juicy Fruit for the next time the grandkids visited. Without realizing it as a child, I had proven myself to be the Strategist of the group.

Personality Types

In a September 2004 New Yorker essay, "*The Ketchup Conundrum*," Malcolm Gladwell described the food science revolution that was initiated by a man named Howard Moskowitz. In 1986, the Campbell's Soup Company tasked Moskowitz to help them determine what the perfect tomato sauce was. At the time, Campbell's Prego brand was in a head-to-head battle with Ragu, which by all accounts was an inferior tomato sauce.

Typically, in the food industry at the time, food manufacturers would hold focus groups to ask consumers what they wanted in their spaghetti sauce; however, Moskowitz was not your typical food scientist. He instead had Campbell's come up with 45 different kinds of tomato sauce that varied in, among

71

other things, chunkiness and tomato flavor. Moskowitz then proceeded to let consumers rate the various sauces on a scale of one to one hundred. At the time of the study, there were only two variations of spaghetti sauce available: regular and spicy. Moskowitz's study found that nearly one third of people preferred a third and non-existent variety: extra chunky.

Spaghetti sauce manufacturers, up until that point, were only offering consumers an authentic Italian style spaghetti sauce, because after all, that was the "best" spaghetti sauce—the way it was supposed to be. In the spaghetti sauce industry's haste to provide authentic spaghetti sauce, they had completely missed out on one third of the market. The reason for this was simple: they assumed that everyone was created equal when it came to their taste in spaghetti sauce. However, much like people have different personality types that they can be classified into, they also have different taste profiles that they can be grouped into as well.

In the same way that you cannot make a spaghetti sauce that is the perfect spaghetti sauce for everyone, you cannot force fit everyone into the same financial strategy either; this is why personality types play such an important role when it comes to personal finance.

While reading the previous story about the interactions between my grandfather, my cousins, and myself, you probably found yourself either relating to or identifying people that you know as similar to one of the kids in the story. The story is designed to describe the four personality types of personal finance that all people can be categorized into and that are the foundation of how we make financial decisions. It also begins to develop the idea of a fifth personality type that is the theoretical ideal; this becomes possible when an individual understands their own personality type.

Of the initial four personality types, there is not one that stands out from any of the others as either superior or inferior to the others. Each personality type has its own strengths and weaknesses, and it is how these traits are understood and managed that determines an individual's financial potential.

Someone who understands their personality type understands exactly what motivates them, what their strengths are, and what their weaknesses are. Understanding these aspects puts you on the path to developing a financial strategy that will not only work for you, but will allow you to thrive financially.

In order to identify your financial personality type, you must first understand what the four core personality types are, and then you must be honest with yourself about who you are and how you make financial decisions. Do you make impulse buying decisions, buy on credit regularly and let debt accumulate, hoard money like it is going to rain for the rest of your life, spend money like there is no tomorrow, or perhaps even have trouble making any kind of financial decision at all? If so, this is the time to acknowledge such traits so that you can build a bulletproof financial strategy.

By reviewing the five cousins story and the descriptions below, you should be able to identify yourself as one of the four core personality types. Keep in mind that everyone will carry various traits from each of these personality types, and not all of the characteristics for the personality type that corresponds to you will necessarily apply to you. What you are trying to identify is the one that describes you best, the one that reveals itself when money is most abundant or most scarce or in times of financial stress or uncertainty.

The four core personality types are the Spender, the Saver, the Scrutinizer, and the Struggler. Understanding which one of these four is your primary personality type will help you become the fifth and most ideal personality type, which is the Strategist.

Review each of the following lists of characteristics to determine which one is your primary personality type.

Spender Characteristics:
- Financial decisions are black and white
- Has the ability to save money
- Often suffers from buyer's remorse
- Often has difficulty maintaining the money they have saved
- Tends to be an impulse buyer
- Needs to see instant or fast results when investing
- Typically does not have a lot of debt
- Can tend to not have a lot of savings
- Often willing to accept more risk when investing
- Can show signs of discipline

Saver Characteristics:
- Makes financial decisions based on emotion
- May tend to worry about money
- Often unwilling to part with money out of fear
- Prefers low risk when investing
- Typically a deal seeker
- Often very disciplined
- Sometimes classified as "cheap"
- Hates debt

Scrutinizer Characteristics:
- Often suffers from "paralysis by analysis"
- Must understand all aspects of their finances
- Often has trouble sticking with a single strategy, al-

ways looking for the next best thing
- Can make irrational decisions through misunder-standing
- Typically will not trust others to help them make the decision
- Must decide for themselves
- Typically very disciplined

Struggler Characteristics:
- Reckless spenders
- Flashy – typically interested in gadgets, fashion, fancy cars, or material goods
- Always needs to have the next big thing
- Will turn to debt in order to acquire now rather than later
- Very rarely saves any money
- Most financial effort spent paying down debt
- Shows complete lack of discipline
- Often stressed about money or current financial situation

Your Personality Type

Now that you have determined which personality type best describes you, you can begin to understand the best type of strategies for your type. Once you understand how to develop these strategies, you are on your way to becoming a strategist. If upon reading these descriptions you are still unsure what your primary personality type is, then read on until it becomes clear.

Spender

Spenders are results driven people, which can make them

75

the easiest to motivate of all the personality types when it comes to money. If you can identify a result or a goal for a spender that they are passionate enough about, getting them to follow through on a strategy is easy.

The primary question spenders have to ask themselves when implementing a financial strategy is, "what do I want out of this?" If a spender can answer this question, they are well on their way to succeeding financially. This is evident in a typical spender's ability to save money in order to make significant purchases. For example, it is not uncommon to hear a spender declare, "I am saving to buy…" The fact that they are saving not borrowing the money differentiates them from a struggler, who would just buy the item on credit for instant gratification. Furthermore, the spender is different from a saver in the way that while they do save, they have an end goal in mind: to spend their money. In most cases, the spender's goals are short term, with a desired result as their motivation.

The key to building a long-term financial strategy for a spender is to set long term goals that have rewarding milestones built in along the way—something like save one million dollars over the next 25 years with rewards built in at different intervals. For example, for the first $10,000 saved, there could be a reward that allows the spender to buy something they really want for $500. At $25,000, there could be reward of spending $1,000, at $50,000 perhaps a reward of $2,500, at $100,000 a reward of $5,000, at $500,000 a reward of a new car, and so on. The key is to give the spender enough motivation to hit the milestone goals so that they build up to the achievement of the final long-term goal.

Another key aspect to consider for a spender is the locking in of results. Spenders often have a tendency to impulse buy, which means that money set aside for growth, can end up being spent. For a spender, the best investment vehicles are the ones that do not allow money to be spent easily. These can be investments that have a penalty for redemption, an RRSP that incurs taxes if redeemed, or even accounts that require a second signature in order to cash out. For a spender, the harder it is for the money to be spent, the better. Don't let this need to secure the money overshadow the emphasis on results, however, because if a spender gets focused enough on a goal, they will do anything to reach it, which makes safe guards almost unnecessary.

Even with the best safe guards in place, a spender can lose course if they don't have clearly defined goals or if they don't see results right away. This is why milestones are so important to spenders and also why it is okay to change the rewards if they no longer motivate the spender. For example, if the original reward is a $1,000 Hugo Boss suit, but half way to $10,000 the spender decides a $1,000 iPad is really what he wants, then it is okay to make the swap. What is important is that the value of the reward remains the same, but the reward itself becomes whatever motivates the spender the most at that price point.

To summarize a Spender:
Primary Motivator:
- Results

Best Financial Strategies:
- Use financial vehicles that deter redemption or spending
- Create milestones that lead up to long term goals
- Strategies that provide results
- Leverage for the right borrower

Saver

If a spender is a results oriented bull, the saver is a delicate flower. Primarily motivated by emotions, the saver is the polar opposite of the spender and the only personality type that will forfeit their own self-interest to work with other personality types. For the saver, money is never about results, attention, or analytics; it is about how the saver feels about their strategy and also how they perceive others to feel.

The most important question savers need to ask themselves when designing their financial strategy is, "how will this make me feel?" Good feelings, bad feelings, and the feelings of others will all play into the decision making process and the commitment to a financial strategy. Where a spender might be motivated to be a millionaire because it will allow them to buy things, a saver, on the other hand, will be motivated to be a millionaire because of how they expect their feelings to change upon achieving the goal. If a spender feels as though they will be happy, stress free, loved by everyone around them, and able to help those in need, then they will be motivated to reach the goal. If, on the other hand, they associate any negative feelings to their financial strategy, they will put the brakes on and fail to follow through.

The greatest deterrent to any strategy for a saver is fear. Most savers for this reason will almost always choose a fixed rate mortgage, even if it is obvious that a variable rate mortgage will save them money. They simply cannot deal with the fear that stems from having a mortgage where the rates could increase. Savers, for the same reason, will gravitate towards secure, low return investments or even pay off debt to pay less interest before they will take any sort of risk trying to earn interest. Savers will shy away from stocks, and for the most part, they will also steer clear of owning a business to avoid the stress and emotions that result from not having a secure job, unless of course they associate strong feelings with the business they are in. The best strategies for a saver are simple, secure, and risk free.

To summarize a Saver:
   Primary Motivator:
   •   Security/emotions

   Best Financial Strategies:
   •   Low risk investments
   •   Accelerated mortgage payout strategies
   •   Strategies that provide certainty
   •   Creation of a "security bucket" with money set aside for emergencies

Scrutinizer

The scrutinizer is a financial architect, an investment engineer, and a mortgage mathematician. The irony is that architects, engineers, and mathematicians are most often the real life professions of this personality type.

Scrutinizers are analytical by nature and will dissect every aspect of a mortgage or an investment in order to determine for themselves if the strategy is the most effective one possible. Their ability to analyze can be a great strength and an equally great weakness, which means the most important question scrutinizers must ask themselves is, "am I overanalyzing this?"

Due to their tendency to overanalyze, the scrutinizer can be the hardest personality type that a financial services professional has to deal with. Their desire to run the numbers themselves and understand every last detail often leads to paralysis by analysis. Frankly, even the best intentioned scrutinizer will more often than not fail to have the background knowledge needed to make the right decision independent of good advice. Their tendency to over complicate and dismiss others opinions can ultimately be fatal to their financial success.

On the other hand, a scrutinizer, who is both willing to take advice and who fully understands their strategy, has the most potential to become a great strategist. The reason that they have so much potential is due to their ability to analyze options and make decisions that will move them forward instead of backwards. A scrutinizer, for example, is the most qualified personality type for a leverage strategy because they will understand the risks, the benefits, and the commitment necessary to be successful.

Scrutinizers also tend to be the most successful when it comes to sticking with a strategy, which is in part due to their stubbornness with respect to numbers and in part due to their tendency to only make a decision when they are absolutely positive that they have picked the best solution. A scrutinizer who fully understands their chosen strategy will in a sense become married to it, which will make it very hard for anyone, including themselves, to deter them from following through to the finish. Furthermore, in a relationship, a scrutinizer has the unique ability to act as the architect and the implementer of a strategy, which can encourage a spouse of another personality type to follow through more effectively than if they were on their own.

To summarize a Scrutinizer:
Primary Motivator:
- Complete understanding/knowledge

Best Financial Strategies
- Clear and easy to understand

- Easily compared to other options
- Strategies that are consistent over long periods of time
- Leverage for the right borrower

Struggler

There are few better ways to describe a struggler than the one who must be the center of attention. Strugglers typically have the best attitudes, are the friendliest people, and generally stand out in the crowd. They have a unique desire to be liked by everyone they come into contact with, and in some cases, they are considered eccentric. As a result of their desire to be both seen and liked, strugglers have a tendency to spend and borrow money to buy things like gadgets, cars, clothes, or even gifts for others to fulfill those desires.

The most important question strugglers must ask themselves when developing a financial strategy is, "will the pleasure I get out of buying this now, outweigh the pain I am going to feel later when I actually have to pay for it?" In most cases, the answer to that question is no; whether or not the struggler wants to acknowledge that fact is another story. This denial tendency makes structure in a financial strategy extremely important.

Access to credit is the first thing that must be cut off for a struggler. Credit to this personality type is like alcohol to an alcoholic. They may think that they can handle it, and they may convince themselves that they are under control. However, it is a slippery slope back to where they started. Dept payoff strategies are the first and best steps to take with this type of individual. Focus on paying off bad debt, and then paying off good debt. Then, if there is money left over, it should be put into some sort of investment that is extremely hard to liquidate.

Similar to the spender, the struggler needs to be rewarded for good behavior, and the best way to do that is with public praise or displays of success. The struggler will always gravitate towards fancy things, and milestone goal setting with rewards that feed this appetite will be beneficial. A further enhancement to this type of goal setting for the struggler is to encourage the fancy rewards that they can be proud of, but that are also assets that will not depreciate very much in value—things like art, vacation properties, or classic cars.

To summarize the Stuggler:
Primary Motivator:
- Things

Best Financial Strategies
- Debt payoff
- Accelerated mortgage payoff
- Anything that locks their savings in or discourages spending

The Strategist

If there were a hypothetical perfect personality type, it would be a perfect hybrid of the four core personality types. The perfect financial personality would have the drive of the spender, the analytical power of the scrutinizer, the positive attitude of the struggler, and the selflessness of the saver. There are very few people in the world however, that even come close to this ideal. As a result, the rest of us must settle for the next best thing, and that is to become a strategist.

The strategist is a person who fully understands their own personality type, understands the personality type of their partner, if they have one, and builds their financial strategy around their own strengths and weaknesses. They do not jump on the financial product bandwagon of some guru financial planner just because everyone else they know is. No, the strategist gets it. The strategist knows that the right financial plans for others may not be the right ones for them.

Recently in the mortgage industry, there has been one product that has been sold as the quintessential mortgage planning product: the Smith Manouvre. The Smith Manouvre is a leverage strategy that has certain tax advantages. Mortgage brokers and real estate investment companies have been selling this product to anyone who has 20% or more equity in their homes, as the end-all financial product. However, their enthusiasm for this product has not disclosed the risks associated with the product, nor has it encouraged people to reflect on whether the strategy is the right strategy for them.

In the right hands, like in the hands of a spender or a scrutinizer, the Smith Manouvre can be a phenomenal strategy. However, in the wrong hands, it can lead to financial suicide. A strategist will be able to recognize almost instantly if this type of product is right for them. A struggler who becomes a strategist will recognize that leverage (borrowing money to invest) is a horrible strategy for them because it provides additional access to credit. A saver turned strategist will realize that the fear of losing the money invested may be too stressful for them. The scrutinizer and the spender may recognize the opportunity, and with consideration, they will accept the risk while at the same time putting safe guards in place so that they do not get too carried away. In all of these cases, the four personality types would be proving themselves as strategists by virtue of being able to make the right decisions for themselves, avoiding the flavor-of-the-week strategy that they otherwise may not have recognized as right or wrong for themselves previously.

Much like fitness and diet plans, it is often too easy to come up with the right plan for the wrong person, which is why understanding personality types is so important. In the same way that asking a person who spent the majority of their life inactive to run a marathon is ridiculous, so too is asking a saver to take all of their hard earned money and invest it in the stock market or asking a struggler to pay off all of their debt and stop borrowing cold turkey without any safe stops in place. You simply cannot ask somebody to follow through on a strategy that they are not prepared to handle or that their core personality traits will not permit, which is why understanding your core personality type, and gravitating towards being a strategist is so important to your financial future.

To summarize a Strategist:

The strategist gets it – they get what motivates them, what scares them, their strengths and weaknesses. The strategist understands their own personality types and plans their finances accordingly.

Section 2
The Strategies

6

Floating vs. Fixed
Don't Be Fooled

On March 25, 2001, Moshe A. Milevsky, Associate Professor of Finance at the Schulich School of Business, published a research report entitled Mortgage Financing: Floating Your Way to Prosperity. By his own admission, Milevsky was not the first to study the benefits of floating[2] versus fixed mortgage rates. However, his study would set off a chain reaction of newspaper articles and television news reports that would change the psychology of Canadians when it came to mortgages. It would also lead to a confidence among those in the mortgage and financial services industry that floating rates were the absolute best option for the consumer who wanted to save money. By the fact that all consumers wanted to save money, this lead many to believe that floating rates were therefore the best option for everyone. Everyone unfortunately did not agree, including Milevsky.

Up until Milevsky's study, the "existing folklore and advice," as he puts it, on floating versus fixed rates were rarely put to any sort of test. Most people who ended up choosing float-

---

2   For the purposes of this chapter, the words floating, variable, and adjustable are interchangeable.

ing rates did so for two reasons. The first reason was because interest rates since the early 1980's had been steadily declining, and given the trend, it was presumable that a floating rate would outperform a fixed rate. The second reason assumed that the wisdom of the crowds was correct, and therefore, the fact that a majority of Canadians seemed to be choosing (or promoting) floating rates encouraged their selection.

The existing folklore and advice only gained steam as a result of Milevsky's research. Mortgage brokers and financial service managers (FSMs) cited the study without knowing its name, who wrote it, or having even read it. Based on a study that few had even read, mortgage professionals unequivocally assured clients that if they took variable rate or adjustable rate mortgages, they would save money. Further, these same professionals pushed their clients with the guarantee that they could lock into a fixed rate mortgage if rates started to rise, not understanding that rising rates had little to do with the effectiveness of a floating rate strategy.

Contrary to what many mortgage professionals believed, Milevsky's study did not guarantee that a consumer would save money by choosing a floating rate over a fixed. It also did not ever take into consideration the prospect of trying to time the market by locking in rates if they were about to rise. (A study on optimizing this practice would be intriguing.) Milevsky's study dabbled in probabilities, particularly of saving money over any given 15-year amortization while maintaining either a floating or a fixed strategy throughout the entire term. In other words, he figured out what the probability of savings was by starting on day one with a floating rate mortgage and staying in that type of mortgage until the very last day of the mortgage's amortization.

What Milevsky determined was that a floating rate mortgage starting on any month between January 1, 1950, and January 1, 1985, with an amortization of 15 years had an 85% likelihood of saving more than $11,351 per $100,000. Conversely the study determined that there was a 10% chance that a mortgage of the same criteria would lose at least $8,393. More precisely the study determined that the average savings for a floating rate mortgage was $22,000 per $100,000 and the floating strategy had an 88.6% probability of success.

The effectiveness of a floating rate strategy seemed to have little to do with the direction of rates—rates were rising for far more than 50% of the 50 years studied—but more to do with the spread between the prime rate and fixed rates around the start date of the mortgage. In the small amount of cases where fixed rates were a better choice, the prime rate was actually higher than the fixed rates at the beginning of the mortgage.

Milevshky's study almost immediately created a problem caused by the fact that few who cited it had actually read it, and even worse, most who cited it made incorrect presumptions with respect to why a floating interest rate saved borrowers money. Most presumed that saving money with floating rates was directly correlated to trends in the direction of interest rate movement. In actuality, it had everything to do with the spread between fixed and floating rates near the start of the mortgage. Even top economists fail to recognize this differentiation almost nine years later.

On October 23, 2009, Douglas Porter and Benjamin Reitzes of BMO Capital Markets wrote in Focus, the weekly economic research digest, that "fixed rates were advantageous during only two recent periods—through the late 1970s and in the late 1980s; in both cases, ahead of a period of rising interest rates, as is the case now." This quote implied that when rates are on the rise, fixed rates are a better choice. What the report failed to acknowledge, however, was that during both of these periods an anomaly occurred in which prime rates had risen higher than fixed rates as a result of the Bank of Canada's desire to slow the economy. The Focus article failed to acknowledge the fact that at the time of the article, prime rate was substantially lower than the five year fixed, which makes today's interest rate environment substantially different than that of the late 1970s or 1980s, contrary to what the above quote would lead you to believe. The two times where fixed rates were advantageous were the only two times in history where prime rate rose above fixed rates for a substantial amount of time; however, they were not the only two times in which interest rates were on the rise. In fact, interest rates rose steadily from 1950 to 1978 without there ever being a period where fixed rates were advantageous. Fixed rates during this period were not advantageous because prime rate was never higher than the fixed rate.

Whether rates are on the rise or not does not matter; what matters is the spread between the fixed and floating interest rates. Historically, this spread has been 135 basis points (1.35%) in favor of floating rates. In the late 1970's and 1980's, the spread favored the fixed rates. In June of 2011, the spread between the best available 5-year fixed rate and the best available floating rate mortgage was 184 basis points (1.84%), to the favor of the floating rates. One can pretty much rest assured that if the prime rate is substantially lower than the fixed rate at the time of financing, then a floating rate mortgage will fare better over time unless prime rate rises drastically higher than its fixed rate counterpart. The only likely time that this would happen would be if the economy became overheated and inflation went through the roof. If the economy gradually recovered, however, and inflation remained manageable, it is unlikely that prime rate would rise above the five year fixed rate. Furthermore, rates would have to increase by almost 5% for a client to be worse off in a variable rate than a fixed.

Why do people go fixed then?

If it appears to be the case that 86.6% of the time a floating rate mortgage will be advantageous to a fixed rate mortgage, then why doesn't everyone go the floating route? It turns out that the decision between floating and fixed is not simply a case of making the statistical bet that is most likely to save you money. Risk plays a major role in the choice a borrower makes as well.

To help one understand the risk versus reward aspect of floating versus fixed rates, we can use a comparison between stocks and GICs (Guaranteed Investment Certificates) to explain. Think of the floating rate like a stock. Over the long term, stock market indices statistically have higher returns than GICs—similar to the way in which floating rates statistically have greater savings than fixed rates. If a person buys high quality blue chip stocks in a diversified portfolio and does not panic when there are normal fluctuations in the market, for the most part, they will be better off than someone who invests solely in GICs. In the same manner, someone who takes a floating rate strategy and sticks to it even when rates rise will most often end up better off than those who chose a fixed rate strategy.

A GIC on the other hand is more like a fixed rate. It locks you in for a certain term so that you do not have to worry about interim market fluctuations. It is safe and secure, and there is little to worry about. Unfortunately by investing in GICs as opposed to stocks, you give up the potential for greater returns. Much like fixed rates, there is a premium on security.

In April of 2004, Milevsky followed up his 2001 research report with an article entitled "Mortgage Financing: Should

91

You Still Float? Four Answers." In the article, Milevsky outlined four types of borrowers based on different risk tolerances. Before we get to that, however, there are two important facts to point out. The first is that, at the time, the Bank of Canada's overnight rate was 2%. At this time, Milevsky predicted that rates would not likely go lower, although there was the outside possibility that they may. We now know that this outside chance has become a reality, and the overnight rate started 2010 at 0.25%. The second point to note is that even though he did not think rates could go much lower, he still wrote the following: "Lenders prefer to make loans for shorter periods of time, while borrowers favor longer term commitments. Thus, in order to induce lenders to give up their precious funds for longer, the 'equilibrium' interest rates on longer-term loans tend to be higher to compensate for the longer 'lock up'. Ergo, borrowers who are willing to accommodate the banks desire to retain control of the funds and agree to shorter term loans, will gain an edge in the long-run."

Even though Milevsky believed that rates were more likely to increase over time than decline, he still believed that floating rates would be more beneficial than fixed rates. This prediction was based on the spread between fixed and floating rates still being enough to give floating rate mortgages the advantage. His previous study, he reaffirms, was not about trying to predict where interest rates would go but about risk management for those faced with the decision between fixed and floating rates. Milevsky then goes on to describe the four types of borrowers and the type of mortgage strategy best suited to them.

The first borrower type is the first time homebuyer. The first time homebuyer is the borrower who is normally the most risk averse, or at least should be. Given that they are new to homeownership and the expenses that go with it and, in many cases, just barely make the income necessary to qualify for their mortgage, first time homebuyers should strongly consider a fixed rate mortgage strategy to secure their payments for at least five years. Those who put a minimum down payment of 5% when purchasing a property or who are near their maximum debt servicing limits should also strongly consider a fixed rate mortgage, as a fluctuation in mortgage payments for this type of borrower can be devastating if not prepared for.

The second type of borrower Milevsky outlines is the risk-averse worrywart. The worrywart is the type of borrower who watches interest rates wondering at every slight fluctuation if they should lock in. The worrywart is the most likely person to make a mistake by choosing a floating rate because they have a tendency to panic and lock in at the wrong time. Much like an amateur investor who tries to time the stock market, the worrywart has little to no chance of locking in at the right time, and they will likely lose sleep trying to do so. For some people, it is just not worth the stress involved. A more secure strategy for the worrywart might be to take on a Scotia STEP or Merix 50/50 type product, where a portion of their mortgage is fixed, while another portion is floating. By taking on this type of strategy, a worrywart would be able to take on an acceptable amount of risk, which would relieve some of the stress associated with going completely floating.

The third type of borrower Milevsky describes is the seasoned veteran. The seasoned veteran is the type of borrower who more than qualifies for their mortgage and has a reasonable amount of equity. In this borrower's case, given that they are less risk averse than their worrywart counterpart and more than able to absorb any fluctuations in payments that may arise as a result of rising interest rates, they should strongly consider a floating strategy. The seasoned veteran may also choose to make payments well above what their actual mortgage payments may be in order to pay off the mortgage much quicker. As an added bonus, the more they pay off in advance of an interest rate increase, the less effect an increase will have on their monthly payment.

The fourth and final borrower Milevsky describes is the financially savvy arbitrageur. Interestingly enough, the strategy Milevsky outlines for this type of borrower has not garnered much attention from lending institutions. This lack of attention is because it encourages a borrower to take out a floating open mortgage at one lender, while simultaneously seeking a 120-day fixed rate hold at another lender. If rates increase over the four month period, the borrower is able to move their mortgage to the second lender at yesterday's interest rates by using the rate hold. If the rate remains the same, the borrower simply reapplies for the rate hold and starts the process over again. This type of strategy would likely result in an annoyed lender and would require caution that the borrower's credit did not get damaged due to multiple credit bureau inquiries. If one chose this strategy, it would be imperative that every time the rate hold was renewed there would be no additional credit check. It is also important to note an increase in interest rates does not guarantee that rates won't decrease again in the future. Such an occurrence could make this strategy less effective than simply selecting a floating rate strategy long term. One's crystal ball would have to be exceptionally clear for interest rate arbitrage to work.

When helping a client choose between fixed or floating rates, I often ask them one simple question, "Will the prospect of your interest rate and payments rising keep you up at night?" This question is typically a good indicator of a person's ability to deal with the potential risks of a floating rate mortgage. It also gives us a pretty good indication of what type of borrower they are. A hesitation is often a sign of risk aversion.

People, as a general rule, have a greater propensity to save money that they have earned than to spend money that they have not. In more simple terms, people will tend to take a fixed rate mortgage so that they are not risking their earned income, as opposed to taking a floating rate mortgage that may or may not save them money, no matter how high the savings may be. Some people just like to know exactly how much their mortgage is going to cost them, plain and simple.

In the cases where a client seems to be a good candidate for a floating rate strategy, I may do a little bit of coaching, but ultimately, the decision lies with the borrower. One thing that we do make sure clients realize is that fixed rates are not a cure for payment shock, the concerns that arise when payments do increase. In fact, there is a chance that a fixed rate mortgage can result in greater payment shock five years down the road when a mortgage comes up for renewal and interest rates have increased drastically. A borrower who chooses a floating strategy, however, may feel this rise in payments gradually over time, allowing them to deal with it in small steps rather than in one big step at the end of the term. On the other hand, that five-year period of time might help one prepare more thoroughly as well. Of course, there is always the chance that rates stay pretty much the same and neither party has to worry about payment shock. The point is that choosing between floating or fixed rates is about understanding your personal risk tolerances and making an informed decision that best suits your needs.

Payout Penalties & Floating Rates

There is another important point to consider in the fixed vs. floating debate: payout penalties. In the last two years, as a result of declining fixed rates, some borrowers have faced astronomical payout penalties. The reason these payout penalties have been so high is because of what is called the Interest Rate Differential, or IRD. An IRD comes into play on a fixed rate mortgage when a client tries to break their mortgage prior to the end of the term and the current interest rate at the time of breaking the mortgage is lower than the original rate. When this occurs, the borrower is responsible for paying the bank the difference between the rate they originally borrowed the money at and the rate that the bank can lend that money for now.

For example, let's say that the bank gave you a fixed mortgage at 5% for five years. On year three, you decided to break the mortgage because you wanted to refinance the property (or wanted to sell it). The current rate at the time is 4%, meaning that if you repaid the bank, they would only be able to lend the money back out at 4%—1% less than what you had originally agreed to pay. Since you originally agreed to borrow the money for 5% for five years, in effect guaranteeing that interest to the bank, you would be responsible for paying the bank a lump sum equivalent to 1% interest for two years.

This problem compounds itself when borrowers deal with certain lenders who calculate their IRD in a manner that is less beneficial to the client and more beneficial to the lender and its investors.

In comparison, a floating rate mortgage avoids any payout penalty issues by typically charging only three months interest.

Floating Rate Protection Strategy

If you are considering a floating rate strategy and can afford to make additional payments every month (which you should be able to because banks always qualify you for a higher rate than the current floating rate), have the bank set your payments at the qualifying rate. For example, at the time of writing, a floating rate mortgage is priced at 2.20%. The qualifying rate is 5.39%. If you were to have the bank set your payment based on the 5.39% rate, you would be able to shorten your amortization and also lower your principal balance. Some banks will also let you re-borrow the money that you paid in advance or skip payments.

You may also choose to put the difference between the actual payment and the qualifying payment into a tax-free savings account. Any bank can set up an auto-transfer so that the money is automatically moved and invested (hopefully in a secure investment) in a Tax Free Savings Account (TFSA). If your payments ever increased beyond what is comfortable, you could then withdraw the money in order to subsidize your payments. Think of this as a floating rate rainy day fund. Chances are that you will never need to use it, but it's nice to know it is there. We will discuss this concept further in the next chapter.

7

 **Mortgage Arbitrage -
Using the Bank's Money to Make
You Money**

In economics, there is a concept known as arbitrage. In simple terms, arbitrage is the ability to take advantage of differences in market prices in order to make a profit. For example, suppose there were two markets for cigarettes, British Columbia and Alberta. In British Columbia, a package of cigarettes costs $7, and in Alberta, the same package of cigarettes costs $10. The difference in price represents an opportunity to participate in arbitrage. By buying a package of cigarettes in British Columbia for $7 and selling it in Alberta for any amount higher than that, you would earn a profit. Voila, arbitrage!

A more interesting example of arbitrage comes from the Economist magazine, which publishes annually The Big Mac Index. The theory behind The Big Mac Index is that if you take a product that is available nearly everywhere in the world in an identical form and compare the price that is paid for that product, you can establish the purchasing power of a country's currency. For example, if in Sri Lanka a Big Mac costs the equivalent of $1.86 USD, and in Norway a Big Mac costs the equivalent of $7.20 USD, you could buy Big Macs in Sri Lanka and sell them in Norway for a profit, discounting, of course, the potential transportation and health safety issues. In both the case of cigarettes across provincial boundaries or Big Macs across international boundaries, the concept is the same: to take advantage of an opportunity to earn a profit.

Arbitrage, however, may not always be as simple as identifying a price difference and then acting upon it. You have to look for opportunities that may not seem obvious on the surface; otherwise, everyone would be profiting from arbitrage. While it may not always seem evident, there are many instances where arbitrage is possible in the mortgage market. Two particular instances can be found in amortization and interest rates.

In both interest rate and amortization arbitrage, one can borrow money at a low interest rate, say 3%, and invest it at a higher interest rate, say 5%. However, unlike in leverage, where you borrow a large sum of money and invest it all at once, in mortgage arbitrage, you use the difference in payments to invest consistently and slowly over the long term. In the case of amortization arbitrage, for example, you could use the difference in payments between a 25-year and a 35-year mortgage, or in interest rate arbitrage, you could use the difference in payments between a variable rate and a fixed rate payment. The key is the realization that there is more to paying off your mortgage than just selecting the shortest amortization, and that effective arbitrage can mean the difference between saving tens of thousands of dollars in interest and accumulating millions of dollars in wealth.

Amortization Arbitrage

Amortization arbitrage is a concept that I stumbled upon several years ago when trying to help a family friend understand the differences between taking a longer or shorter amortization. At the time, the federal government had just introduced

40-year amortizations to the Canadian Mortgage and Housing Corporation's (CMHC) product lineup. The primary concern for most people with respect to the 40-year amortization was the interest costs associated with taking an extra 15 years to pay off your mortgage. At a 4.00% interest rate, the total interest paid on a 40-year amortization was 72% more than the interest you would pay on a 25-year amortization. On a $300,000 mortgage, a client who took a 40-year amortization as opposed to a 25-year amortization would pay an additional $125,466 in interest assuming that the interest rate remained 4% for the entire life of the mortgage.

For the majority of people, there was one of two lines of thinking. The first was, "there is an ice cube's chance in hell that I will pay 72% more interest on my mortgage, sign me up for 25 years." The second rationale was, "sweet, I can save $330 a month! I'll take the 40 year!" Obviously, the word save in this case was being confused with the concept of paying less money towards principal, the client was in reality not saving money, just deferring payment until later. The latter was obviously the more dangerous of the two lines of thinking. Those excited about saving $330 a month had usually already spent the monthly savings before they had even acquired it. The former, while much more conservative and substantially safer, was the choice of most financially savvy borrowers, but it turned out that there was a third option that had the potential to build substantial wealth over the life of a mortgage. That option was, and still is, amortization arbitrage.

Amortization arbitrage is the simple practice of investing the difference in payments between a longer and shorter amortization. In our $300,000, 4.00% interest example, the difference in payments between a 25-year and 40-year amortization is $330. By taking advantage of that difference in payments and investing the $330 monthly at a rate of 6% a total of $632,598 would be accumulated over 40 years, a far greater amount than the additional $125,466 that would be paid in interest, this is a very suitable way to take advantage of the longer amortization products on the market.

Amortization arbitrage works with any combination of amortizations, which is important because as of October 15, 2008, most lenders no longer offer 40-year amortizations, although they are still available in some cases. The longest amortization now available in most cases is 30 years. While the potential to accumulate wealth using a 30-year amortization is not quite as good as with a 40-year, the potential is still there, and the benefits get better as the returns on your investments go up. Since there are many 35 year mortgages out there, we will use 35 years and 25 years for the purpose of this example. The difference in interest paid between 35 and 25 years on a $300,000 mortgage at 4.00% is $81,994; the difference in monthly payments is $256. Over the course of 35 years, the potential returns on $256 invested monthly are as follows:

- At 2% annual return $155,242
- At 4% annual return $231,132
- At 6% annual return $353,354
- At 8% annual return $552,026
- At 10% annual return $877,028
- At 12% annual return $1,410,774

Even at a mere 2% annual return, the $256 has far more value being invested than it does going towards paying off the mortgage. The savings in interest on a 25-year amortization are a paltry $81,994 compared to the $155,242 return at the end of the 35-year period. As the rate of returns gets bigger so do the benefits. At a 12% rate of return a 35-year amortization is the difference between being a millionaire and just having a house that is paid off.

One may think that if you were earning 4.00% on the difference in payments, or paying 4.00% on the mortgage, you would end up earning the same amount that you saved in interest payments. As you can see, however, this is not true. Amortization arbitrage works even in the cases where your rate of return is equal to your mortgage interest rate; this is a result of two forces working against each other: the forces of diminishing and exponential returns. When paying off your mortgage, the amount that you are paying interest on is always getting smaller. With each payment, the principal you owe is tapering and so is the interest cost, which means the returns are diminishing. When investing, on the other hand, growth is exponential because not only are you adding extra principal to your investments, but you are also earning interest on the interest. It is fact that even at the exact same interest rate, exponential returns will always earn more money than diminishing returns will save you.

The astute reader may ask, "would you be better off if you paid your mortgage off in 25 years and then invest the full mortgage payment at the end of 25 years for ten years?" The answer is that it depends on the returns of the investments. For a $300,000 mortgage amortized over 25 years at 4.00%, the monthly payments would be $1578. If you were to invest $1578 over ten years, you would get the following returns:

- At 2% annual return $209,583
- At 4% annual return $232,244
- At 6% annual return $257,631
- At 8% annual return $286,065

- At 10% annual return $317,900
- At 12% annual return $353,529

When you compare the returns on the full mortgage payment invested for ten years versus the difference being invested for 35 years, there is a sweet spot around 4.00% where you break even. However, if you garner any sort of return higher than 4.00%, there is a huge benefit to investing over the long term.

Since it is far more likely to average greater returns over a long period than a shorter period, and given the much greater potential of long term investing, amortization arbitrage becomes a no brainer. Furthermore, short-term investing has its pitfalls; if you were to hit a ten year period, like 1999 to 2009, your returns would be dismal. If you could average those poor ten years with the previous 25, however, you would be in much better shape.

The most important factor to consider in amortization arbitrage is the potential momentum of the money over the long term. As you can see, if you get a 4% return, it doesn't really matter which strategy you choose—other than the fact that with the arbitrage strategy, you would always have cash on hand for a rainy day. On the other hand, if you get lucky and get a 12% return over 35 years, you would be better off to the tune of $1.1 million.

Practicality plays an important role as well. Average returns being potentially higher over the long term and money momentum aside, we can't forget to mention the fact that an individual is more likely to stick to investing a smaller amount over the long term than to save a large amount over the short term. Let's face it, if you aren't willing to save and invest $256 now, the chances that you will be willing to save $1,578 in 25 years is slim to none. Furthermore, having a safety net of $256 a month is a far better option than having a house that has a little more equity, a higher payment, and no cash on hand at all should an emergency arises.

Interest Rate Arbitrage

We already know from previous chapters that money grows faster than it saves, which is reason enough to participate in both amortization and interest rate arbitrage. We also know that 88.6% of the time a variable rate mortgage is going to save you money. Why, then, do so many people choose fixed rate mortgages? The primary reason is for the security of knowing what your payment is going to be for the next five years. Security, it seems, is worth paying for.

The primary problem with a fixed rate mortgage however, is that if fixed rates are higher than variable rates, which they usually are, you are paying the bank interest that you don't need to be. As one of my colleagues likes to say, "Why on earth would you pay the bank more than you have to?"

One might argue that in a variable rate mortgage there is a chance that you could end up with a higher rate, and as a result, pay more interest by the end of the term. However, we have already determined that the direction of rates does not affect the saving power of a variable. This is especially true when you consider that the opportunity for the greatest savings is at the beginning of the mortgage when you owe the most money, which is why taking a variable rate mortgage, even when there is the expectation that rates will rise, will save you money.

So, if lack of security is the reason most people don't pick variable rate mortgages, the question then is how can we make them more secure? The answer is interest rate arbitrage.

Interest rate arbitrage is a simple, yet highly effective,

strategy. All you do is determine what your payment would be at the current five-year fixed and variable rates respectively, and then, you set up an automatic investment of the difference every month in a safe and secure investment.

For example, if the five-year fixed rate was 5% and you had a mortgage of $300,000 amortized over 30 years, your payment would be $1,601.07. If the variable rate was 3.5% your payment would be $1,342.91. The difference between the two mortgage payments would be $258.16, which would be the amount that you would automatically invest every month.

If your interest rate rises and you find that it is not affecting your quality of life or whether or not you can pay your bills, you keep storing the $258 away. If, on the other hand, you start to stress because your interest rate and payments got too high, then you use the money to subsidize your mortgage payment.

The benefit of this strategy becomes apparent when you are able to continue putting the money away without dipping into it to subsidize your payments. At a return of 8%, for example, you would accumulate the amounts indicated in the amount saved column. Compared to taking the 5-year fixed rate, it becomes obvious that a variable rate mortgage with interest rate arbitrage set up is the superior choice.

What you will notice is that around year 20, the amount you have saved by putting away $258 a month is roughly equal to the amount left owing on your mortgage, effectively knocking 10 years off of your mortgage. In year 21, you become free of your mortgage. Alternatively, if you chose not to pay off your mortgage and continue investing until the end of the mortgage, you would have a paid off mortgage and $365,745 in the bank. Combined with amortization arbitrage and accelerated bi-weekly payments, the returns would be even higher.

$300,000 mortgage at 5% over 30 years
vs. 8% return on $258 a month

	Amount saved	Balance Owing
5 Years	$18,941	$275,285
10 Year	$46,771	$243,648
15 Years	$87,663	$203,150
20 Years	$147,746	$151,309
25 Years	$236,029	$84,948
30 Years	$365,745	$0

The combination of both strategies and accelerated bi-weekly payments would look like this. The payment that the savings would be based on would be a 25-year amortization at 5%, $1744.81, the actual payment to start would be based on a 30-year amortization at 3.5%, $1342.91, for a difference of $401.90. For simplicity's sake, a $402 monthly investment would earn the following amounts with an 8% return.

$300,000 mortgage at 5% over 30 years
vs. 8% return on $402 a month

	Amount saved	Balance Owing
5 Years	$29,512	$266,092
10 Years	$72,875	$222,687

15 Years	$136,591	$167,125
20 Years	$230,209	$96,001
25 Years	$367,766	$4,956.90
30 Years	$569,881	Paid off year 26

By using both interest rate arbitrage and amortization arbitrage together, your mortgage strategy would help create a nest egg of $569,881.

8

 Debating Mortgage Insurance - When Paying $10,000 for Insurance is Good

The debate over mortgage insurance started for me many years before I was even legally capable of buying a house. I was one of the indoctrinated. From an early age, I understood that mortgage insurance was the devil. One would have to be out of their mind to pay for insurance that protected the bank, not oneself, especially at prices of thousands, if not tens of thousands of dollars. Not to mention that there would be interest on that premium and on the extra money I needed to borrow in order to put less than 25% down. It was clear to me that the only way to buy a house was with 25% cash up front (the requirement at the time, now 20%).

In fact, the first condo I ever bought, at the ripe old age of 20, was bought with a 25% down payment. That 25% was hard earned money that I accumulated scrubbing golf clubs, waiting tables, and investing like a madman. You would have thought that given my investment savvy at such a young age I would have realized what I know now: the opportunity cost of putting that 25% down payment on that condo far exceeded not only the insurance premium that I so desperately tried to avoid, but also the interest on the insurance premium and the

109

extra money that I would have needed to borrow to make a 5% down payment instead.

It wasn't until well after I made this mistake that I met a man that would later become a mentor of sorts: Fred Sarkari. Fred always had a different way of looking at things. A motivational speaker and coach by trade, he was great at asking questions and thinking outside the box. His outside-the-box thinking and prodding lead me down a path one cold snowy day that changed my views on mortgage insurance forever.

The day it all happened is clearly etched in my memory. Fred and I were meeting for one of our weekly lunches, enjoying our favorite sushi restaurant's famous love boat, which was always ordered with the clear distinction that we were two completely straight men who were not in love but who loved the happy hour price of sushi in the form of a small wooden ship. As we sat and chatted about, among other things, my future career as a mortgage broker, Fred asked an odd question, "What do you think about mortgage insurance?"

My obvious and very quick response was, "It's the devil."

Fred rebutted by asking if I thought it was bad even for those who could not afford 25% down, to which I agreed that mortgage insurance for most borrowers wasn't a bad thing. However, I was certain that for those who had the means to avoid it, it was most certainly a rip off.

Fred, for whatever reason, wasn't so sure. He asked, "What would you lose by putting 25% down instead of 5%?"

I responded quickly and confidently with, "Nothing."

He prodded again, "Are you sure?"

"Yes, absolutely!"

It took him a while, but Fred finally got me to realize what he was talking about: the opportunity cost of the additional money needed to avoid mortgage insurance. Quite simply, Fred was trying to figure out if it was worth putting down $80,000 to save $10,000. The result of this conversation was a whole new way of looking at the costs and benefits of mortgage insurance.

How Much Does Mortgage Insurance Really Cost?

There are three aspects that must be considered in order to determine the cost of mortgage insurance: the insurance premium, the interest on the insurance premium, and the interest on the additional money borrowed in lieu of putting a higher amount down. The insurance premium is easy to calculate based on the following mortgage insurance premium table.

Mortgage Insurance Premiums

Loan to Value Ratio	Premium on Total Loan Amount
Up to and including 85%	1.75%
Up to and including 90%	2.00%
Up to and including 95%	2.75%
Add 0.20% for every 5 years of amortization beyond the 25 year mortgage amortization period	

Based on the above chart, it is simple to determine that on a $400,000 home purchase with 5% down (mortgage of $380,000) the insurance premium would be $10,450 ($380,000 x 2.75%.)

The second factor in determining the cost of mortgage insurance is the interest on the insurance premium. You may be wondering why there is interest on the premium? Quite simply, because most people who put less than 20% down on a house, also need the insurance premium capitalized (included) in the mortgage amount. A $380,000 mortgage with the premium included would give a final mortgage amount of $390,450.

Assuming an interest rate of 5% and an amortization of 25 years, the interest on the insurance premium would total $7,783, giving us a total premium and interest cost of $18,233.

The third aspect to consider is the interest on the additional money borrowed at 5% down. On a $400,000 purchase, one would need an $80,000 down payment in order to avoid mortgage insurance—$60,000 more than the minimum. The interest on the additional $60,000 at 5% over 25 years would amount to $44,689.

By adding up the insurance premium, the interest on the insurance premium and the interest on the additional funds borrowed, the total cost of having an insured mortgage over an uninsured mortgage would be $62,922.

Based on the $62,922 cost, simple math would be enough for most people to determine that mortgage insurance is in fact the devil. Putting $60,000 down to save $62,922 seems like a no brainer. At least this is the logic that has lead to so many people having the preconceived notion that one should avoid mortgage insurance at all costs. It is the exact same logic that led me to believe that mortgage insurance was a negative set of words. This type of thinking, however, has proven to be short sighted.

The question should not be "how much does mortgage insurance cost me?" It should be "how much can mortgage insurance make me?" The answer to that question is what changed my beliefs on mortgage insurance all together.

If you isolate the $60,000, understanding that not putting it down on your mortgage would cost you $62,922 in interest over 25 years and figuring out what it could earn you over 25 years, you would likely be surprised to find the following: $60,000 invested over twenty-five years would earn you the following amounts based on the following annual rates of return:

Rate of Return	$60,000 after 25 years
4%	$159,950
5%	$203,181
6%	$257,512
7%	$325,646
8%	$410,909
9%	$517,385
10%	$650,082
11%	$815,128
12%	$1,020,004

As you can see, even with a rate of return that is lower than the interest rate on the mortgage, $60,000 has more earning power than it does saving power, but of course we already knew this. At the end of a mortgage term, a borrower who insured their mortgage would have paid $62,299 more in interest, but would have anywhere from $159,950 to $1,020,004 more money in the bank, depending on the annualized rate of return on their investments. Which borrower would you rather be?

The Other Side

Financially astute readers would point out that there would be a difference in payment between the insured mortgage and the uninsured mortgage, given that the former mortgage amount would be $390,450 and the latter $320,000. Based on the $400,000 purchase price, 25-year amortization, 5% interest rate example, that difference would be $409.74 per month.

One might ask, "what would the returns on $409.74 invested monthly look like at similar rates of returns, and would one be better off putting the extra $60,000 down, avoiding the mortgage insurance and investing monthly instead? The answer to that question depends on two things: the rate of return and the likelihood of sticking to a monthly investment.

When you compare the returns of $60,000 invested up front over 25 years and $409.74 invested monthly over 25 years, choosing the better option depends on the rate of return that you expect. As you can see from the chart below, at any rate of return less that 7%, one would be better off investing $409.74 monthly. At rates of return of 7% or higher, it is much more beneficial to pay the mortgage insurance and keep the $60,000 invested instead of putting it towards a mortgage. It is also worth noting that the potential upside of having the $60,000 invested from day one is far greater than the potential downside of not being able to make at least 7%. The upside potential is the first of several reasons why the insured mortgage strategy makes the most sense.

$60,000 invested One Time
vs. $409.74 Invested Monthly for 25 Years

Rate of Return	$60,000 over 25 Years	$409.74 Invested Monthly Over 25 Years
4%	$159,950.00	$209,178.35
5%	$203,181.30	$240,977.07
6%	$257,512.24	$278,451.93
7%	$325,645.96	$322,658.24
8%	$410,908.51	$374,846.96
9%	$517,384.84	$436,500.26
10%	$650,082.36	$509,373.10
11%	$815,127.83	$595,542.20
12%	$1,020,003.86	$697,463.33

There are several other reasons that the insured mortgage strategy makes more sense than trying to avoid mortgage insurance. They include the fact that having $60,000 invested is an insurance policy against job loss or financial hardship that is second to none. In addition, having a lump sum invested from day one is much easier to maintain than a monthly savings plan, as unforeseen cash flow needs could encourage one to discontinue a monthly savings plan.

While this strategy may not work for everyone, namely those who need to put more money down to qualify or those who only have a minimum down payment, there is little reason to avoid mortgage insurance other than the misunderstanding of the costs and benefits. It is clear from a numbers standpoint that taking out a mortgage that is insured can be a far superior alternative to avoiding mortgage insurance by liquidating one's investments.

9

Accelerated Pay Down - How To If You Are Going To

The one concept that we have not covered up until this point is accelerating the payment of your mortgage. We have spent most of our time discussing how to use your mortgage opportunistically in order to build wealth and how you must possess the right type of personality and have the right amount of discipline to even entertain these strategies. For those who won't feel comfortable leveraging their house in order to create a balanced portfolio of debt and investments, there is always the good old method of paying down your mortgage as fast as possible.

If you have ever had a mortgage with a major bank, you are probably aware that they often give you the option to do three very important things in order to pay your mortgage off faster. First, banks usually give you the option to select accelerated bi-weekly or weekly payments. Second, most banks offer you the option to increase your payment amount by a specific percentage every year. Third, most banks will let you pay a certain percentage per year without penalty towards the principle of your mortgage. If you are going to pay down your mortgage as fast as possible and not use any of the strategies previously detailed, then having these options is essential. In the event that paying down your mortgage as fast as possible is the option most suited to your personality type, I also recommend having some sort of readvanceable component built in. In other words, if you are going to focus on paying off your mortgage with every penny you have, make sure that every penny you put in is a penny you will have access to later if you need it.

When your financial strategy relies solely on debt payoff without saving, you open yourself up to the risk of running out of savings should you unexpectedly need a reserve of cash. If a small leak in the roof turns to a mold problem and eventually leads to a $50,000 remediation bill, your shingles need to be replaced, or your condo assesses you in order to top up the reserve fund, you can find yourself in a financial jam even though from a debt standpoint you have done all of the right things.

There are several good examples of mortgage products that will allow you to access paid off funds even if the unthinkable happens. Firstline Mortgage's (Owned by CIBC) Matrix product, the Scotia Step program, the National Bank All In One Mortgage and the BMO Bank of Montreal Mortgage Cash Account all provide access to payments made in excess of the normal payment schedule. Each of these three products has unique features that may be suitable for you, depending on your financial situation.

Accelerating Your Payment
Accelerated Bi-weekly or Weekly Payments

Accelerated payments can help you pay off your mortgage substantially faster than monthly or semi-monthly payments. On a typical 25-year mortgage at 6%, bi-weekly payments would help you pay off your mortgage four years and eleven months sooner. The savings come from making the equivalent of an extra monthly payment every year.

Here is how it works. If you were to theoretically split each monthly payment into 2 payments (semi-monthly), you would have 24 payments per year. If you opted to pay bi-weekly, your payment would be the same amount as the semi-monthly payment; however, you would be making that payment every two weeks for a total of 26 payments per year. In monthly terms, you would be making 13 payments every year as opposed to 12, which is why your mortgage gets paid off so much faster.

Given the effectiveness of bi-weekly payments, many people infer that weekly payments would fair even better. They do, but not as much as you might think, because weekly payments are still the monthly equivalent of 13 payments, on a $300,000 25-year mortgage at 6%, like the one above, the savings by paying weekly would only be $585.90 more than bi-weekly. That is $585.90 over 25 years, a rather inconsequential amount. Weekly payments instead of bi-weekly payments is more a matter of convenience than savings, and this is an option I often recommend to self-employed or commissioned sales people whose incomes are subject to fluctuations.

One of the best ways to determine your mortgage broker or financial service reps payment acceleration IQ is to ask them the question "does your mortgage get paid off quicker if you pay bi-weekly versus weekly?" If they answer that it does get paid off faster, but don't mention the insignificance, inform them of their mistake and search for a more qualified person to assist you with your mortgage.

It is also important to ensure that your payments are actually accelerated and not just adjusted to weekly or bi-weekly. The simplest way to determine if a payment is accelerated is to compare it to the monthly payment. If the bi-weekly or weekly payment is exactly half or one quarter of the monthly payment, it is accelerated. If it is anything less, it is not.

Increasing Your Payment

In addition to selecting bi-weekly or weekly payments, I also recommend that my clients review their current mortgage situation annually. When we do an annual review, I not only look for ways to save the client money by rearranging their mortgage, but I also encourage them to increase their payment by at least 5% every year, using their payment increase option. This practice gradually increases the client's payment without causing a payment shock, and it can save a client tens of thousands if not hundreds of thousands of dollars over the life of their mortgage. It is a simple practice that will pay off dividends.

Lump Sum Payments

Lump sum payments are the most obvious and fastest way to pay off your mortgage. Opportune times to make lump sum payments can be plentiful or few and far between, depending on your personal circumstances. The most frequent opportunities can be when you receive a bonus at work, receive a refund on your taxes, make a little bit of extra money on the side or from overtime, receive an inheritance, or win the lotto. Obviously, the more often you can make lump sum payments, the faster you will pay your mortgage off.

Bonus Chapter

Dirty Little Mortgage Secrets (Its Not All About Rate)

I wish to leave you with a few parting words of advice. Those words are simply this, STOP FOCUSSING ON RATE! While it may seem counterintuitive, this small piece of advice may very well save you one day from making a mistake that could cost you thousands, if not tens of thousands of dollars. It is the focus of the consumer on rate that has caused many lenders to strip their mortgages of features, and caused a large amount of pain for many mortgage borrowers. As a result, there are several dirty little secrets you should now be aware of when you borrow money.

Most people would agree that if you borrow money from a lender or a bank, you should be able to pay it back whenever you like. However, due to the extreme pressure for banks to lower rates, some lenders have begun to feel differently. Some lenders think that if you borrow money for a term of five years at historically low rates, you should have to continue to borrow that money until the term expires or until you sell the home that the mortgage is secured against. I imagine this is because if you don't have a mortgage, they don't make money.

You might be surprised that there are cases where a mortgage lender will try to prevent you from paying off your mortgage in full. They prevent this by putting some creative clauses into their mortgages that most borrowers won't find out about until it is far too late. In some cases, these clauses are for a portion of your mortgage term, perhaps three of the five years, and in some cases, they are for the entire term of your mortgage. Either way, does it seem right for a lender to make you keep a mortgage that you can afford to payout? Furthermore, is it right for your lender to ensure that you are obligated to earn them income, while your wealth is depleted? I don't think so. People borrow money because they need it; if they no longer need it, they should be able to pay it back.

What is worse is that these clauses prevent you from refinancing or switching lenders. Why is this important? Well, let's say you have a $400,000 property that you made a $100,000 down payment on. At the time of your purchase, you had the financial ability to make that large down payment. Unfortunately in life, people's circumstances change. Let's say you lose your job, become ill, or for some other reason need to access the equity in your home. Should you not have a right to refinance to get a portion of your money back in your pocket? I am sure you will agree that you should.

Don't think for a second that these types of clauses are limited to small financial institutions either. Recently, several large banks have begun offering no frills mortgages with these types of clauses in an attempt to lure new clients in with the promise of lower rates. What is the best way to avoid ending up with a lender that has these clauses? Deal with a mortgage planner who has experience and the ethical standards not to place you with this type of lender. That means not just dealing with any mortgage broker; it means dealing with the best, which also means not chasing rate.

Chasing rate is a term that mortgage brokers like to use for people whose only concern when looking for a mortgage is that they get the best rate. It does not matter to them that 3.99% at one lender can be more expensive than 3.99% at another lender. Quite frankly, this focus on rate can be one of the most costly mistakes a mortgage borrower can make. The right way to look at any mortgage is to look at the straight dollars and cents of a mortgage. The actual amount that the mortgage is going to cost you at the end of five years.

You are probably wondering how it is possible that 3.99% at one lender can be cheaper than 3.99% at another lender. Well, this is simple and complicated at the same time. The simplicity of the matter is that it all has to do with the terms of the mortgage. This means the fees, the compounding, and the renewal process of the lender. It also has a lot to do with the payout penalty calculations of the lender. Lenders have all kinds of ways of calculating payout penalties. The simplest of these, and also the most standard, is the three-month interest penalty. This penalty is exactly as it sounds: three months' interest. There is another kind of payout penalty however that is less understood.

The Interest Rate Differential, or IRD, is the method of calculating the lender's loss associated with you paying off your mortgage early. Simply put, if you agreed to borrow at 5% for five years, and you payout your mortgage after 2 years, you have to pay the lender the difference between the rate you borrowed the money at and the rate they can lend it at now. If the current rate is 4%, you owe them the equivalent of 1% interest over three years. IRD only comes into play, however, if there is a loss for the lender. If the bank can lend the money out at a higher rate, then you only have to pay the three month interest penalty because the lender is actually going to realize more

123

profits from you breaking your mortgage.

The problem with the IRD is that different lenders calculate them in different ways. Some lenders use comparable posted rates; some use comparable discounted rates; some compare to the rate closest to the remaining amount of time left in your term; and some lenders use bond market rates in their calculations. If you do not know how the calculation works going into your mortgage, you can end up with a huge payout penalty without ever knowing that your mortgage was any different than your neighbor's, who may have a substantially lower payout penalty.

Why is your payout penalty so important? How many people do you know that have sold their house on the exact day that their mortgage came up for renewal? If the answer is zero, then you understand that unless you have an open mortgage, you are almost always going to have a payout penalty to deal with.

A couple years ago, one of my clients took out a mortgage with a lender that calculated their IRD using the bond market rate. Initially, I advised the client against that particular lender because of this practice, but the client was interested in the slightly lower rate that the lender offered. The client assured me that this was going to be their lifelong home and that they would not be paying out the mortgage early. Six months later, the clients, who had emigrated from the UK, were threatening to walk away from the mortgage and move back to Europe, outside the reach of any prosecution. Why? Their payout penalty was $43,000. It should have been closer to $7,000, and it would have been had they chosen a different lender. The question is, how do you avoid these lenders? The answer, once again, is deal with an experienced and ethical mortgage planner.

On the bright side of things, many of the lenders who once sold rate in exchange for the inability to pay out mortgages and higher payout penalties have disappeared. Given their odd mortgage practices, they were unable to compete or sell their mortgage backed securities, leading to bankruptcy or dissolution. This leads us to our next and final point: be careful of the lender that you deal with because they may not be around when your mortgage comes up for renewal. Orphaned mortgages are going to become more and more common in the next couple of years. These are mortgages where the closure of a lender causes a mortgage not to be renewed. As we said earlier, peoples circumstances change, and even though you may have been able to qualify for your mortgage originally, it does not mean that you will qualify when it comes up for renewal. In most cases, if you deal with a major bank, your mortgage will automatically be renewed, assuming that you have never missed a payment. If your lender no longer exists, however, there is no chance you will be able to auto renew. Consequently, if your circumstances have changed and you are unable to obtain a new mortgage, you may be forced into selling your home.

The list of other possible restrictions that you may incur in exchange for a lower rate goes on and on. These include but are not limited to.

- Inability to break your mortgage before the term is up
- A penalty surcharge for breaking your mortgage within a certain time frame
- "Reinvestment fees"
- Interest rate differential (IRD) penalties calculated in a way that benefits the lender
- Inability to move mortgage from one house to another unless the transactions both close on the same day

- High lock in rates on variable mortgages
- Inability to refinance within a certain time frame
- Amortization restrictions
- Minimum amortizations
- Penalties on otherwise open lines of credit
- No pre-payments within 30 days of discharge
- Inability to move mortgage to another province
- Excessive administrations costs
- Limited pre-payment privileges

The best way to avoid all three of these situations is to deal with a highly experienced, ethical mortgage planner who deals with strong, credible lenders who offer competitive rates and full service mortgages.

Set Forth Into the Future

Dirty little secrets aside, you are now prepared to step into the world of mortgages with more knowledge than most people ever scratch the surface of. Armed with an understanding of why the advice of previous generations will not do you justice, you can set forth looking for opportunity rather than savings. You can pick a mortgage planner based on sophistication rather than just rate. You can assess your personality and design your mortgage strategy around your strengths while protecting against your weaknesses. You can choose now to exploit your mortgage rather than allowing your mortgage to exploit you.

Recommended Reading

David Chilton
The Wealthy Barber

Bob Burg & John David Mann
The Go-Giver

Thomas J. Stanley & William D. Danko
The Millionaire Next Door

T. Harv Eker
Secrets of the Millionaire Mind

Napolean Hill
Think and Grow Rich

Douglas Gray
Mortgages Made Easy

Fraser Smith
The Smith Manoeuvre

About the Author

Nolan Matthias, Lead Planner and Co-Founder of Mortgage360, is the best selling author of *The Mortgaged Millionaire* and *Golf Balls Don't Float*.

With an acute business sense, an educational background in economics, and a strategic understanding of mortgages, Nolan is quickly becoming one of the Canadian Mortgage Industry's brightest stars. Through a processed and thorough approach he helps his clients successfully pick the right mortgage to meet their financial needs.

Nolan has served as a subject matter expert for the Alberta Mortgage Brokers Association, been a member of Canadian Mortgage Professional Magazine's editorial board (industry magazine), has written for the Calgary Herald's editorial section, and been a material contributor to the Alberta Mortgage Associate Program (MAP) licensing course.

Nolan has the unique privilege of being the youngest mortgage associate ever invited to join Mortgage Architects as a Lead Planner, an honor only bestowed upon the most successful and well respected mortgage brokers in Canada.

Financial Coaching

The best athletes in the world all have coaches, as do the most successful business leaders, even Bill Clinton looked to the most famous personal and business coach in the world during his impeachment hearings. Yet the one place where there isn't nearly enough coaching is in the area of finances.

Nolan Matthias' financial coaching program will help you solve whatever financial issues you have today, and help you set yourself up for financial freedom tomorrow.

Benefits include:
- Unbiased second opinion on all financial products
- Monthly and yearly spending analysis
- Monthly and yearly budgeting
- Financial planning and strategy
- Integration of mortgage strategy into your financial plan
- Goal setting and execution workshop
- Net worth analysis
- Net worth diversification strategy
- Debt reduction planning
- Debt payoff prioritization

Please note that there is an approval process and waiting list for coaching services, with priority being given to existing Matthias Financial Inc. mortgage clients.

Call 1-866-615-6132 or visit nolanmatthias.com for details.

mortgagedmillionaire.ca

Visit mortgagedmillionaire.ca for access to the
financial calculators used to write this book,
as well as access to updated content and
the Mortgage360 Insider newsletter.